INVESTOR'S GUIDE
TO
LIMITED PARTNERSHIPS

David F. Windish

New York Institute of Finance

LIBRARY OF CONGRESS
Library of Congress Cataloging-in-Publication Data

Windish, David F.
     Investor's guide to limited partnerships / David F. Windish.
        p.   cm.
     Includes index.
     ISBN 0-13-737370-8 : $21.95
     1. Limited partnership--United States. 2. Limited partnership-
  -Taxation--United States.   I. Title.
KF1380.W56 1988
343.7306'62--dc19
[347.303662]
                                                    88-22761
                                                        CIP

This Publication is designed to provide accurate and authoritative information in regard to the subject matter covered. It is sold with the understanding that the publisher is not engaged in rendering legal, accounting, or other professional service. If legal advice or other expert assistance is required, the services of a competent professional person should be sought.

From a Declaration of Principals Jointly Adopted by a Committee of the American Bar Association and a Committee of Publishers and Associations

© 1988 by NYIF Corp.
A Division of Simon & Schuster, Inc.
70 Pine Street, New York, NY 10270-0003

Printed in the United States of America
10 9 8 7 6 5 4 3 2 1

New York Institute of Finance
(NYIF Corp.)
70 Pine Street
New York, New York 10270-0003

Contents

Chapter 3

WHAT YOU SHOULD KNOW ABOUT LEGAL ORGANIZATION AND STRUCTURE, 29

Chapter 4

WHAT YOU SHOULD KNOW ABOUT PARTNERSHIP TAXATION, 45

Chapter 8

Chapter 9

Appendix A

Appendix B

Preface

In recent years, an investment alternative has been as readily available to the average investor as common stock. This alternative is the limited partnership. Unlike common stock, however, information and guidance on the limited partnership investment vehicle has been relatively scarce. The purpose of *Investor's Guide to Limited Partnerships* is to fill this gap.

The book concentrates on "public limited partnerships," which the author feels will be of most interest to most investors. Limited partnership interests are securities, just like stocks and bonds, and when offered for sale to the public, the offering and securities must adhere to the same laws as stock offered to the public. The same distinction exists between public offerings of stock and private placements and public offerings of limited partnership interests and private placements.

Despite the emphasis on public limited partnerships, anyone interested in private placements also should find *Investor's Guide to Limited Partnerships* valuable and informative.

CHAPTER **1**

Introduction

You have \$5,000 to \$10,000 to invest. In deciding how to invest this money, you will consider several possibilities and the various advantages and disadvantages of each, as well as your own personal and financial situation. For instance, you may consider an insured deposit at a bank or a savings institution. Money invested in this manner is protected through a federally backed insurance program and your rate of return is fixed through the agreement between you and the bank or other institution. In short, you know that at the end of a certain period of time, barring some major national financial catastrophe, you will get back your original investment plus some fixed additional amount.

The advantages of a bank deposit are readily apparent, but so are the disadvantages. While your principal is protected and your rate of return fixed, your return is limited. It can never be more than the rate provided in your deposit agreement. If you are willing to accept more risk, you may be able to increase your return. You may choose to invest in common stocks.

Common stock offers the potential of unlimited return offset by the potential for the total loss of your investment. Of course, in practical terms, most common stocks never reach their potential in either direction. You, as an investor, will limit your potential loss by careful study of the company in which you intend to invest. You will weigh the risks of a decline against the potential for growth. Advice on how to invest in common stocks is readily available and books on the subject number in the hundreds, if not the thousands.

In recent years, another choice has been as readily available to investors as common stock, but unlike common stock, information and guidance on this form of investment has been relatively scarce. This investment is participation in a limited partnership in which units are offered to the public in a public offering in much the same fashion as stock may be offered to the public.

This is not to say that these three choices are the only ones available. On the contrary, there are many possibilities. Rather, the point is to highlight that most investors know very little about limited partnerships as an investment choice. This lack of knowledge can mean one of two things—either the investor is missing out on potential investments that could enhance his wealth or making ill-advised investments that are more likely to result in losses than in growth.

The purpose of this book is to fill this gap, to make you aware of the public limited partnership as an investment vehicle, and to acquaint you with its advantages and disadvantages.

What Is a Limited Partnership?

As its name implies, a limited partnership is first and foremost a *partnership*. This concept of "partnership" is extremely important, and you must never lose sight of this. Your inclination may be to equate an investment in partnership units with an investment in shares of corporate stock. As we shall see, the two types of investment are very different, and your rights as an investor, as well as how your share of income is determined and distributed, are not the same for an investment in a limited partnership as for an investment in a corporation.

As a beginning, let's define a "partnership" as simply an association of two or more persons for the purpose of carrying on a business for profit as co-owners. The partners contribute either money or services to produce income. The partners, in effect, are agreeing to work together to set up and operate some type of business or money-making enterprise. The heart of this business association is the agreement between the partners, whether that agreement is reduced to a formal written contract or merely the result of a friendly handshake. Of course, a public limited partnership always will be governed by a formal written contract.

From the agreement to carry on a business together, partners are automatically assuming certain rights and obligations. If the partnership is not a limited partnership, that is, if the partnership is a "general partnership," all the partners share equally in the right to conduct the business of the partnership. Any partner who is tending to partnership business automatically binds the partnership by his acts. This means that any one partner can obligate all partners, and all general partners are jointly and severally liable to third parties for the business acts of any partner.

All general partners are also jointly and severally liable to third parties for the acts of agents and employees of the partnership. Each partner is liable for the full amount of any third-party claim. Should a partner pay off a valid claim, there is a right of contribution. The paying partner can require the other partners to contribute their share, but the third party is free to seek redress from any one of the partners.

Obviously, if every investor could be personally liable for the debts and obligations of the partnership without limit, the partnership would not make an attractive investment vehicle. The concept of limited liability was introduced to make an effective form of business organization, the partnership, attractive to investors. A "limited partnership" is nothing more than a general partnership in which one or more partners have their liability limited in much the same fashion as shareholders in a corporation have their liability limited. Limited partnership status cannot be acquired without filing and recording a certificate of limited partnership.

In a limited partnership, there must be at least one general partner. The general partner or partners manage the business and are personally liable for the obligations of the partnership. The rights and obligations of the general partners in a limited partnership are the same as those of the partners in a general partnership. The limited partners in a limited partnership are exempt from partnership liability for the debts, obligations, and losses of the partnership as long as they do not participate in the management of the partnership. In other words, the most a limited partner can lose in a partnership is his investment, just like a shareholder in a corporation. This limited liability is what makes the limited partnership attractive as an investment vehicle.

You must be careful not to equate a limited partnership investment with an investment in common stock. To obtain limited liability in the partnership, you must give up any say in management. Limited partners, unlike shareholders, are not entitled to a vote on business matters and have no say in selecting the management of the partnership. This is not to say that limited partners are without any rights, but their rights are much more limited than those theoretically exercised by shareholders. We will look at this subject more closely in Chapter 3, which deals with what you should know about the legal organization and structure of limited partnerships.

Development of Partnership Investments

The growth and development of the limited partnership investment vehicle can be traced back to the first real mass marketing of tax shelters that occurred in the early 1970s. In a real sense, the early history of limited partnership investments is the history of tax shelters. Today, limited partnerships may still offer tax advantages in the right situations, but thanks to voluminous tax reform legislation enacted in recent years, the main emphasis on partnerships has shifted from tax shelter to enhanced investment return in the form of current cash flow.

Just why limited partnerships have been used to attract investors and how they have been used will be taken up in Chapter 2.

A relatively recent development in the limited partnership field has been the formation of what are termed "master limited partnerships." Essentially, a master limited partnership is a limited partnership in which interests are publicly traded through listings on a stock exchange or in the over-the-counter market.

Some master limited partnerships were formed when a promoter gathered together units from various partnerships under one roof. For example, investors with limited partnership interests in different oil drilling ventures may have exchanged their interests for an interest in a new limited partnership made up of all the interests contributed. Interests in this new entity would then have been listed on a stock exchange and the investors would have achieved a degree of liquidity that they did not have prior to the formation of the master limited partnership.

Master limited partnerships also have been created by corporations spinning off part of their operations into new limited partnerships. The spun-off portion of a business or activity could then provide the benefits of partnership taxation (which are not available to investors as shareholders) to investors as limited partners. In most cases, master limited partnerships formed in this fashion were expected to be income generators with large cash flows.

Investor interest in master limited partnerships skyrocketed following passage of the Tax Reform Act of 1986, and many new businesses were being formed as publicly traded limited partnerships rather than corporations. The tax incentives appeared very attractive. However, tax legislation at the end of 1987 took away the advantages for many newly formed master limited partnerships. A ten-year grace period was provided for existing partnerships, and certain partnerships, specifically those investing in real estate or oil and gas, were exempted from the new provisions. In any event, with the loss of tax benefits, interest in the formation of new businesses (other than those excepted) as master limited partnerships waned.

We will take a special look at master limited partnerships, especially those investing in real estate or oil and gas, in Chapter 6.

Securities Registration

When limited partnership interests are to be offered to the general public, the offering and the securities (the limited partnership interests) must be registered with the Securities and Exchange Commission (SEC). "Private placements," unlike public offerings, are exempt from full SEC registration, usually because the number of investors will be limited to a few sophisticated investors, or all participations in the partnership will be offered solely within a single state.

A common misconception is that public offerings are somehow "better" than private placements, that SEC registration guarantees the quality of the underlying investment. In no way is this the case. Registration of a public offering with the SEC does *not* guarantee an investment. The registration process merely requires that certain information concerning the investment and its sponsors or general partners be fully disclosed in a prospectus, and that this prospectus be made available to potential investors. An investment in a public limited partnership can be just as good or bad an investment as an investment in partnership interests that are privately placed.

As a general rule, however, the disclosure required for public registration usually provides more information about the limited partnership and its general partners than does the offering circular for a limited partnership when the limited partnership interests are to be privately placed. Often though, this information does not include specific information on the underlying properties or businesses in which the limited partnership's funds will be invested. Many public limited partnership offerings are structured as blind pools. Investors do not know the specific properties in which they are investing but have to rely on and trust to the judgment of the general partners.

The pool of capital or the total amount of money paid in by all investors when interests in a partnership are offered to the public also is usually much larger than the total investment in a private placement. This is the case even though the minimum investment from each investor is usually much smaller in a public offering, usually in the $5,000 to $10,000 range, and even less when the investor is making the investment as a contribution to an Individual Retirement Account (IRA) or self-employed retirement (Keogh) plan.

The larger pool of capital available to the general partners in a public limited partnership has both good and bad points. The size of the public offerings allows investors to gain whatever advantage can be obtained from economies of scale. A large limited partnership, investing in many underlying properties, prospects or businesses, may spread management costs, resulting in a lower per-unit cost.

The size of a public limited partnership also may offer another advantage. With more capital available, the partnership can diversify its underlying investments. For example, if the limited partnership is investing in real estate projects, the partnership may acquire several properties in different locations. This diversification reduces the risk that a limited partner's entire investment will be lost. By the same token, of course, the greater diversity also reduces the opportunity to make enormous profits.

One more point in favor of public limited partnerships from the investor's standpoint is that a great deal of work is done on behalf of the investor by the broker-dealers who are offering the limited partnership interests for sale. The major investment houses all maintain departments that sift through the public offerings that are registered with the SEC. This source of professional advice should not be overlooked by investors.

We will take a closer look at what public registration means to you in Chapter 5.

Taxation of Partners and Partnerships

For tax purposes, a business or investment entity can be only one of the following: a proprietorship (an individual), a partnership, a corporation, or a trust (an estate is treated much the same as a trust). While state law, as noted previously, controls the contractual relationship among partners and their dealings with outsiders, the Internal Revenue Code and the Internal Revenue Service determine whether or not you have a partnership for tax purposes.

For starters, the Internal Revenue Code definition of a partnership is very broad. A partnership may be "a syndicate, group, pool, joint venture, or other unincorporated organization through or by means of which any business, financial operation, or venture is carried on, and that is not a corporation or a trust or estate."

Considering the broad scope of this definition, it is perhaps more useful to consider what a partnership is not. It is not the mere sharing of expenses or the simple co-ownership of property. What's more, as a general rule, the partnership is not a taxpayer, it is a conduit through which business or investment results are passed to the partners. Although a partnership does file a tax return, the partnership itself pays no income taxes. Each individual partner must report his share of partnership income on his personal tax return and pay taxes based on his individual income tax rate. This tax liability imposed on the individual partners based on their shares of partnership income arises whether or not partnership income is actually distributed to the partners.

This conduit nature of the partnership provides an immediate advantage from a tax standpoint, especially since the Tax Reform Act of 1986 lowered individual tax rates below the tax rates applied to corporations. The total taxes imposed on a business operation operated as a partnership generally will be less than the taxes imposed on the same business operated as a corporation. In the first place, the partnership avoids one layer of taxation altogether, the corporate tax. But even if income is retained and reinvested in the business, the tax paid by partners may be less than the tax that would be paid by a corporation. Accordingly, a partnership can earn income, distribute enough to partners to meet their tax liability attributable to their shares of partnership income, and have more left for reinvestment than if the business or venture were operated as a corporation and the corporation retained all income after taxes for reinvestment.

As noted, this state of affairs led to great interest in the conversion of corporations, or parts of corporations, into master limited partnerships. The threat to federal revenue, however, was quickly noted by Congress, which enacted legislation in 1987 specifically directed at certain partnerships. Under the 1987 tax legislation, a "publicly traded partnership" is treated as a corporation. Note that this treatment applies to *publicly traded* partnerships and not simply *public* partnerships. The distinction is important and will be considered further in connection with the discussion of what you should know about partnership taxation in Chapter 4.

In enacting the rule that taxes publicly traded partnerships as corporations, however, Congress saw fit to create certain exceptions. And these exceptions are important to investors. First, a partnership that was publicly traded on December 17, 1987 (or had taken certain steps toward public trading) is exempt from the rule through 1997. Second, publicly traded partnerships investing in certain activities, notably real estate and oil and gas, are not subject to tax as corporations.

To sum up the tax treatment of partnerships, then, partnerships, other than certain publicly traded partnerships, are conduits and not taxable entities. As for the partners, they are reporting their shares of income or loss directly on their own tax returns. The Tax Reform Act of 1986, however, placed a major restriction on the use of losses from certain investments as a means to defer or avoid tax on income from other sources. Generally, losses from "passive activities" can be used only to offset income from passive activities. Similarly, a tax credit generated by a passive activity can be used only to offset tax liability attributable to a passive activity.

Portfolio income, such as dividends, interest, and royalties, is not considered income from passive activities under this rule. Any loss or credit that cannot be used by an investor because of the restrictions may be carried over to future years and applied to passive income or tax liability attributable to passive income in subsequent years. A loss that remains unused as of the time the investor disposes of the passive investment that generated the loss may be deducted at that time.

For the purpose of the restrictions on deductions and credits from passive activities, an activity generally is a passive activity if it involves the conduct of any trade or business, and if the investor does not materially participate in the activity. In the case of a limited partnership interest, special considerations apply. Since a limited partner generally is precluded from participating in the partnership's business if the partner is to retain limited liability status, material participation is not possible and a limited partnership interest is automatically passive. This means that income, deductions, and tax credits passed through to a limited partner generally are considered passive income, deductions, and credits. An exception, however, is provided for portfolio income earned by a limited partnership and passed through to the partners. This portfolio income is not passive income under the passive loss rules.

Following enactment of the passive loss rules, many saw the master limited partnership as the answer for investors who had invested in tax shelters that were producing passive losses which were no longer deductible against other investment income and earned income. The idea was simple. As limited partners in a partnership producing income, the limited partners would receive income that could be offset by their otherwise nondeductible losses. Of course, the 1987 tax legislation destroyed this strategy for publicly traded partnerships that are now treated as corporations.

What about those publicly traded partnerships that are not treated as corporations under the exceptions? Congress had an answer for this, too. A publicly traded partnership that is not treated as a corporation is subject to a special passive loss restriction that treats each such partnership separately. In other words, losses from a publicly traded partnership may offset only later income from that same partnership. Similarly, income from a publicly traded partnership may be offset only by losses from that same partnership.

While some of the tax concepts briefly introduced here may seem complicated at first, they are important for understanding investments in public partnerships and maximizing return from these investments. We will worry more about these topics in Chapter 4.

Understanding Your Return

No matter what your objectives may be, the true test of any investment is whether it provides a greater return in line with your objectives than other investments. In other words, no investment should be made unless it has the promise of enhancing your wealth and well-being. But how do you go about measuring your return from a limited partnership investment? Many measures of return are available to lead or mislead, and it is the latter that you must be careful to recognize before you invest.

It is not uncommon for promoters and general partners to boost current yields through various "yield enhancement" techniques. Wary investors will learn how to figure their potential return accurately and how to avoid promised returns that are created with blue smoke and mirrors, the slight-of-hand artist's stock in trade. Chapter 7 will show you how.

Other Limited Partnership Matters to Consider

While this chapter has introduced you to the general topics discussed in many of the remaining chapters, there are still other matters to consider.

Chapter 8 will present a concise comparison of the limited partnership investment to other familiar investments. This chapter will compare the limited partnership investment to investments in stocks, bonds, mutual funds, real estate investment trusts, and others. Finally, Chapter 9 will present what you may want to consider in planning your own personal limited partnership investment program, taking into account various possible special situations.

Investing in limited partnerships can be rewarding. The purpose of this book is to help you understand limited partnership investments so that you can make an informed decision on whether a particular limited partnership offers you the opportunity to enhance your personal wealth.

CHAPTER 2

How and Why Limited Partnerships Have Been Used to Attract Investors

Many factors influence investments: factors such as economic conditions, rate of inflation, interest rates, and tax rates applied by federal, state, and local government on income of different types. Investors respond to the changes and seek out investments that offer what they perceive to be the best benefits in light of existing economic conditions and their own personal financial situations.

The period spanning the last half of the 1970s and the first half of the 1980s was a time of generally high tax rates and high inflation. It was during this time that tax shelters and tax-advantaged investments experienced an explosive growth. Battered between the twin scourges of high taxes and high inflation, investors naturally sought out those investments that promised them either tax savings or exceptionally high returns.

In this environment, the limited partnership became the investment vehicle of choice. As a form of business organization, the limited partnership could be used to acquire and operate those assets that were perceived (rightly or wrongly) to offer high returns in a period of high inflation, assets such as real estate, oil and gas, and other natural resources. As an entity under the tax law, the limited partnership could be used to pass tax benefits to investors which they could not obtain through the corporate form of business organization.

Limited Partnership as Tax Shelter

Most tax shelters took the form of limited partnerships because this form of organization provided the combination of the tax benefits of a partnership and limited liability for investors. This was the right combination for an investor in a mass-marketed investment in which other participants were total strangers.

As a partnership, the limited partnership could bring together an individual (or corporation) that has expertise in a specific industry and investors seeking specific tax benefits or specific returns. The partner supplying the expertise would act as general partner, and the investors would be limited partners.

In a tax shelter limited partnership, the general partner would manage the business and assume general liability for the partnership's obligations. Of course, this general liability of the general partner was often more illusory than real, since the general partner was more often than not a corporate entity. The general partner, as manager of the tax shelter activity, would gather the investors' capital, make investments, keep the partnership books, report results, and distribute any partnership profits to the limited partners. Note that while the general partner would make all decisions regarding partnership capital, the general partner itself would contribute little or none of the partnership's capital. Investors, as limited partners in a tax shelter limited partnership, would provide the necessary capital to acquire and operate the underlying assets of the partnership and, to the extent available, would receive the bulk of cash distributions from profits generated by the partnership. While supplying most, if not all, of the limited partnership's capital, the limited partners surrendered any right to participate in the management of the underlying assets of the partnership.

Tax shelter limited partnerships would provide tax benefits to investors because profits and losses arising from the operation of partnership assets would flow through to the individual limited partners. The activities of the limited partnership would be reflected on the personal returns of the limited partners in proportion to their interests in the partnership. In short, tax shelter limited partnerships permitted investors to share in tax benefits as well as profits generated by the underlying assets of the partnership, while allowing the investors to retain the limited liability enjoyed by corporate shareholders.

Just as corporate shareholders, limited partners could realize any income generated by the assets and operations of the business entity, with one additional advantage. Income from the partnership would retain the character of that income when reported on the partner's tax return. For instance, if the partnership realized capital gain or tax-exempt income, the individual partners would report their share of that capital gain or tax-exempt income. If a corporation earned tax-exempt income, that income would lose its character as tax-exempt income and would be taxable as a dividend when distributed to the shareholders.

In most cases, however, the primary goal of a tax shelter limited partnership was not to generate taxable income from the outset of its operations. Rather, tax shelters generally would look to generate tax or paper losses (tax deductions) and various tax credits early in their operations. These tax deductions and credits would be available to the limited partners for use on their personal tax returns to offset highly taxed income from other sources and to reduce their individual income tax bills. The same underlying assets producing tax deductions or credits would not provide a direct tax benefit to investors if the assets were held by a corporate entity. Such tax deductions and credits would remain locked in the corporation and could be used only on the corporation's tax return.

The advantages offered by tax shelter limited partnerships, however, unfortunately led to abuses in two respects by some individuals. Some promoters would either misrepresent the value or extent of the underlying assets that would be acquired by a tax shelter limited partnership. Others would misrepresent or overstate the tax benefits that would be available to the investors. For example, in the field of oil and gas, unscrupulous promoters sold investors on ventures that owned no leaseholds on which to drill for oil and gas. Other promoters pushed various over-appraisal schemes, in which the price paid for assets by the partnership was artificially inflated to support large deductions or tax credits. It was these abuses that, in large measure, finally influenced Congress to pass the legislation that severely curtailed the tax shelter available to passive investors.

How the IRS Inadvertently Encouraged Tax Shelter Partnerships

Perhaps one of the greatest ironies in the history of the development of the tax shelter limited partnership is how the Internal Revenue Service inadvertently encouraged the formation of tax shelter partnerships through its attack on another form of business organization, the professional corporation. Since a partnership is not a taxpaying entity, but a conduit through which income and loss flow through to the partners, the partnership form of organization is an attractive tax shelter vehicle. Merely calling an organization or association a partnership, however, does not necessarily make it a partnership for tax purposes. The Internal Revenue Code and the Internal Revenue Service determine the classification of a business or investment entity for federal income tax purposes, regardless of what the participants choose to call it or how it is classified under state law.

The Internal Revenue Service follows its own regulations in classifying business organizations as corporations or partnerships. These regulations originally were adopted when the IRS was seeking to strike down the formation of professional corporations or associations by reclassifying them as partnerships for tax purposes. At the time, the tax law greatly favored corporate retirement plans over tax-favored retirement plans for self-employed individuals. Professionals such as doctors, dentists, and lawyers could avoid paying an immediate tax on a substantial part of their professional earnings if they could incorporate and have the corporation make contributions to a qualified retirement plan on behalf of the professional "employees" of the corporation. The contributions to these plans were deductible from the corporation's income and were taxable to the professional employees only when drawn out of the plan.

Since the IRS was attempting to reclassify nominal corporate entities as partnerships, the regulations were drawn to slightly favor partnership classification over corporate classification. The way this was done was to list various characteristics possessed by corporations and to treat an organization as an association taxable as a corporation if, after examining the characteristics possessed by the organization, it more nearly resembled a corporation than a partnership. The IRS listed the following six characteristics that pertain to corporations in its regulations:

1. Associates
2. Objective to carry on a business and divide the gains
3. Continuity of life
4. Centralization of management
5. Limited liability
6. Free transferability of interests

Since corporations and partnerships both have associates and the objective of carrying on a business and dividing the gains, the IRS announced that only if an organization possessed more than two of the remaining four corporate characteristics would it be treated as a corporation for tax purposes. Of course, this meant that if an organization possessed only two of these remaining four corporate characteristics, it would be a partnership for tax purposes. In other words, in attempting to gain revenue from professional corporations, the IRS opened the door to the later use of the limited partnership for tax shelter activities.

The following is a rundown of the four corporate characteristics and how they are avoided in a limited partnership.

Continuity of Life. A limited partnership usually calls for dissolution on the death, insanity, bankruptcy, retirement, resignation, or expulsion of a member of the partnership. The remaining partners retain the assets of the partnership and continue the activities of the partnership. The only practical effect of this arrangement is a legal dissolution that prevents the partnership from having the continuity of life that is characteristic of a corporation.

Centralized Management. A limited partnership under the Uniform Limited Partnership Act must have the corporate characteristic of centralized management. This characteristic of a corporation may not be avoided by a limited partnership.

Limited Liability. Since the general partners in a limited partnership provide general liability, this corporate characteristic is avoided, even though the limited partners have limited liability in a fashion similar to that of shareholders in a corporation.

Free Transferability of Interest. Free transferability of interest is the power of the owner of a partnership interest to transfer his entire interest without the consent of other partners. This corporate characteristic is avoided through restrictions on transfers placed in the partnership agreement.

As a general matter, the IRS did not meet with much success in trying to reclassify tax shelter limited partnerships as associations taxable as corporations based on its regulations that favored partnership over corporate classification. It was simply too easy to avoid two of the four critical corporate characteristics. In the end, the IRS eventually conceded that an entity organized under and complying with the Uniform Limited Partnership Act would be treated as a partnership for tax purposes.

Underlying Investments for Limited Partnerships

With the limited partnership providing the form of organization that both permitted a flow through of tax benefits and secured for investors limited liability, there still was the matter of selecting investments or activities that would provide the income or tax benefits sought by investors. Since the limited partnership could be tailored to almost any activity, it is not surprising that the limited partnership became the investment vehicle of choice for a wide range of activities.

While it may be impossible to describe every investment that at one time or another was packaged in limited partnership form, it is possible to summarize those investments that proved most attractive to investors seeking tax shelter. Not surprisingly, many of these same underlying investments remain popular today as underlying investments for public limited partnerships, even though the tax benefits have been reduced in importance and greater emphasis is placed on the production of current income.

It is not our purpose here to provide guidelines on how to select investments or activities that provide the underlying investments for public limited partnerships. Our concern is understanding the public partnership as an investment vehicle. With this in mind, here then is a brief summary of those investments that have been organized as limited partnerships and a brief description of their salient features.

REAL ESTATE

Over time, real estate has proved to be an excellent investment. Continuing inflation and the pressure of demand has pushed up values for real estate of all types, albeit to varying degrees and at different times. Widespread home ownership also has made real estate an investment that more people are comfortable with, since they already have some familiarity with its potential advantages and disadvantages.

The major tax shelter aspect of real estate is that rents may be sheltered from taxation by deductions for depreciation and, to some extent, by interest and other expense deductions attributable to the purchase and operation of a real estate investment. Since depreciation does not require a cash expenditure to produce a tax deduction, rents may produce a positive cash flow without a corresponding amount of taxable income.

In the heyday of tax shelters, another feature of real estate was its ability to produce significant tax losses in conjunction with a positive cash flow. These tax losses could be used to shelter an investor's income from other sources which might otherwise be taxed at rates as high as 70 percent on the federal level alone. Now, of course, this feature of real estate is generally not available through public partnerships. Now, if deductions exceed rents so that a tax loss is created by a real estate investment, the excess loss may not be used to shelter income from nonpassive activities, or income from portfolio investments such as stocks and bonds. Nevertheless, real estate remains an attractive investment in the right situations and tax benefits may still enhance the return an investor receives from income-producing real estate. Let's look at a very simple example.

EXAMPLE. Suppose a sponsor gathers together 500 investors who each contribute $10,000 to construct a project with a total cost of $5 million. Further assume that the project will produce rents of $500,000 per year over and above the expenses of operation. An investor who must pay a combined federal and local income tax rate of 40 percent would net only $600 on his $1,000 share of the annual rent, if the rent were fully taxable. However, of the $1,000 that could be distributed to this investor, only $682 is taxable after reduction for depreciation. With a tax of only $273 on the $1,000 cash flow, the investor's after-tax return on his $10,000 investment is boosted to $727, or 7.27 percent. (This is, of course, a simplified example, but it does illustrate the point that real estate *may* offer attractive returns in conjunction with tax benefits. We'll take a closer look at tax matters in Chapter 4.)

There are, of course, many different types of real estate, including residential properties and commercial properties. More advice probably has been written on how to invest in or buy real estate than on any other investment property, and an investor choosing not to rely solely on the advice of others as to the soundness of the underlying investments of a public partnership investing in real estate should not be at a loss in learning the fundamentals.

Conventional residential real estate may involve the construction or purchase of new apartment buildings or the purchase of used existing properties. There are no government subsidies involved to cover a portion of the tenants' rents, nor is there any government financing for construction of the project. Generally, apartment projects tend to be somewhat more risky than commercial properties, since tenant turnover can create problems.

Government-subsidized housing may be supported either by financing for the project or through subsidies to supplement the rent paid by tenants. Permanent financing for low-income housing is available through various federal agency programs. In addition, states may provide financing for projects, notably through state housing agency bond issues. Local governments may provide tax abatements for low-income housing. The Department of Housing and Urban Development (HUD), under Section 8 of the United States Housing Act, pays the difference between the fair rent for an area and 25 percent to 30 percent of a family's income. These assistance payments are guaranteed for 20 years, but rent guarantees under the Section 8 program were suspended in 1984 for new projects. The subsidies, however, continue for existing properties and may be resumed in the future for new properties. State and local governments also may provide rent assistance to low-income families and individuals. There is also a federal tax credit for the cost of construction, rehabilitation or purchase of low-income housing. This credit, however, is reduced if financing is provided through tax-exempt bonds or supported with other federal subsidies.

Commercial properties or office buildings generally offer a safer investment when compared with residential real estate. One potential problem for an investor in a partnership building or purchasing new commercial space is trying to decide whether tenants will be available when the project is complete. Commercial building seems to run in boom-or-bust cycles, and an investor must answer the question of whether the commercial real estate market is ready for another boom or bust before jumping into a limited partnership commercial real estate program.

There are still many other types of real estate that can serve as the underlying investments for public limited partnerships. *Shopping centers* can be stable, easily managed investments that appreciate significantly as well as produce current income. *Hotels and motels* require management with great expertise in the hotel and motel field.

Perhaps the hottest of real estate ventures for the 1980s has been *adult congregate living facilities* (ACLF) or other special *housing for senior citizens.* The aging population and the special problems of the elderly has spurred the interest in these properties. In addition to the real estate investment, these projects produce income through the extra services provided to the senior citizens, which may range from simple meals in a central dining facility to full medical and nursing care.

OIL AND GAS

United States domestic production of oil remains less than domestic consumption. What's more, world supply is subject to changes that may occur literally overnight. For investors, this means oil and gas exploration and production is a risky business, but at the same time is a business that offers the potential for significant rewards.

The search for oil and gas usually begins with preliminary exploration designed to identify potential oil and gas locations. Once potential sites are located, intensive surveys are conducted to determine whether drilling should actually be undertaken. In the usual situation, the oil and gas operator will acquire a lease from the landowner for potential oil and gas sites. This lease gives the operator a "working interest," also known as an "operating interest," in the oil and gas property. This interest is essentially the right to locate drill sites, drill, and remove oil and gas. In exchange for this bundle of rights, the landowner usually retains a "royalty interest," that is, the right to a share in the proceeds from any production from the property.

Investors generally should be wary of investing in oil and gas programs in which the operator has no leases or rights to acquire leases. Since all rights flow from the lease, investors have no way of knowing for certain whether their money will be invested in land with good potential for oil and gas production without a lease.

As a tax shelter, oil and gas has offered favorable immediate tax treatment with the potential to capitalize on a very valuable commodity. The tax benefits include deductions for intangible drilling costs, although this deduction may be limited for passive investors. More importantly, depletion deductions allow investors to receive tax-free income from producing properties. The current percentage depletion rate is 15 percent of gross receipts from oil and gas production. In short, in computing tax liability on oil and gas income, investors entitled to depletion deductions may deduct 15 percent of their share of gross receipts in addition to any other deductions produced by the investment. Since the deduction is computed on "gross receipts," the reduction in taxable income is usually much higher than the 15 percent rate would seem to indicate.

Many oil and gas programs are structured as limited partnerships, although other forms of business organization are used. Limited partnership oil and gas programs may be divided roughly into various categories according to the nature of the programs and their objectives.

An *exploratory program* is an oil and gas venture organized to drill in an area that has no known production. Exploratory programs present the greatest risks but offer the potential for the greatest rewards. Investors in exploratory programs must expect more dry holes and more unsuccessful programs. Even in a successful program, cash flow may be several years down the road because money from early production may have to be used to finance development.

A *development program* involves drilling new wells in an area of known production. Naturally, there is a higher probability of finding oil and gas than in an exploratory program. Investors should keep in mind, however, that simply finding oil or gas does not mean success. It is relatively easy to find oil or gas with today's modern technology, but whether the find will work out to be profitable is an entirely different matter. If the size of an oil or a gas find does not justify the costs associated with bringing a well into production, investors are just as bad off as if no oil or gas were found.

A *balanced program* is a mix of exploratory and development drilling. How the program is weighted, whether toward exploration or development, tells you to what degree the characteristics of an exploratory program or a development program will predominate.

An oil and gas *income program* is essentially buying already producing properties with proven reserves. Such a program offers no special tax benefits, since deductions for intangible drilling costs or percentage depletion are not available. If you invest in an oil and gas income program, what you are doing is buying a commodity in the ground. Any significant gains, other than an "interest factor" to compensate for the period over which it takes to recover your investment, must come from a rise in the price of oil and gas. Of course, in the meantime, you are at risk for price declines.

EQUIPMENT LEASING

Equipment leasing fills a very important role in our economy. Many individuals and businesses will find that they have a temporary need for additional equipment that does not justify an outright purchase. These individuals and businesses look to rented or leased equipment to fill their needs. In other situations, companies may not be able to use the tax benefits provided by the purchase of equipment. These companies may find that leasing the equipment ultimately will cost less than an outright purchase. In any event, limited partnerships formed for the purpose can purchase equipment that is likely to be leased to receive the rental income as well as any possible tax benefits.

Equipment leasing can involve just about anything. A partial list of equipment that has been leased by limited partnerships includes computers, aircraft, cable TV systems, railcars, ships and barges, shipping containers, medical equipment, and offshore and onshore oil drilling rigs. A twist to the standard equipment leasing arrangement is what is known as a sale-leaseback. A typical sale-leaseback involves a business that sells some of its property or assets to investors and immediately leases the property or assets back.

From the lessee's point of view, the sale of assets followed by their leaseback may be advantageous from a tax standpoint. Tax deductions for rental payments may be greater than depreciation and interest deductions generated by ownership. This is especially true if the property that is the subject of the sale-leaseback has already been fully depreciated or if the property is leased back for a period that is less than its useful life. Also, the sale-leaseback can free up substantial amounts of capital for the seller-lessee.

Regardless of whether leasing is through a sale-leaseback or a straight lease, leasing rather than buying for a business is essentially an additional source of financing. Lessees may turn to leasing to obtain equipment that they might not otherwise be able to obtain. This is especially true when bank credit is not available or difficult to obtain. Through leasing, the lessee avoids restrictive loan agreements that an outright purchase might entail. Also, the lessee obtains flexibility. The lessee knows that it will not be stuck with outmoded equipment and will be able to respond more quickly to changing needs.

From the investor's standpoint, equipment leasing can be a risky investment. Investors in equipment leasing limited partnerships should assure themselves that potential lessees are credit worthy, since the lessees' primary motivation for leasing may be financing. There is also the question of obsolescence. A lessee may lease equipment rather than risk being saddled with outmoded equipment. Technological change can leave a limited partnership holding equipment that no one wants to lease and few are willing to buy, even at greatly reduced prices. Overavailability of equipment owned by the limited partnership can mean that rental income will be less than that projected by the partnership when the investor made his investment.

Simply put, all of these factors point out that the softest number in projections given for any equipment lease investment is likely to be the residual value for the equipment after it can no longer be leased or at the end of the lease program. Nevertheless, it is this residual value that often will determine whether an equipment leasing program will be profitable or not. Investors in any equipment leasing limited partnership must be willing to gamble on the accuracy and reliability of the projections given by program sponsors for residual values.

FARMING

Farming, as a tax shelter, traditionally has provided two forms of tax shelter: tax deferral and the conversion of ordinary income into what had been more favorably taxed capital gain. Tax deferral was achieved through current tax deductions for costs that, in other businesses, would have to be capitalized. The activity for which the costs were incurred would then produce income in a later year, at which time the deferred taxes would have to be paid. In several situations, this later income might have been capital gain.

Farmers are also entitled to special deductions. Many of these deductions are similar to capital improvement costs that might be incurred in any business, but the farmer can take current deductions for these costs rather than recover them through depreciation or amortization over a period of years. The effect is tax deferral. The deductions offset income in the year taken, but the income that results from the expenditures is realized in a later tax period.

Orchards, groves, and vineyards produced tax benefits very similar to crop operations, but the tax deferral was generally for a longer period. Since it requires several years to bring an orchard, grove, or vineyard into production, the longer preproductive period meant a longer deferral period, say four or five years as compared to one year for crop activities.

As an investment for limited partnerships, farms, orchards, and similar activities are not nearly as important as they were during the heyday of tax shelters. A limited partnership engaged in farming today is classified as a farm syndicate, a classification that severely restricts available tax benefits. A farm syndicate can deduct the cost of feed, seed, fertilizer, and similar farm supplies only for the year in which the items are consumed. Also, farm syndicates must capitalize and defer deductions for preproductive period costs relating to all fruit and nut trees and vines. All this eliminates the use of prepaid costs to provide tax deferral in farm operations conducted through limited partnerships.

Considering the real risk in farm operations, few limited partnerships are now formed to engage in farm operations since they cannot offer tax benefits. Nevertheless, where profitable operations are possible, or if the underlying real estate is a good speculative value, a limited partnership may be formed to engage in an agricultural endeavor.

CATTLE AND LIVESTOCK

The purchase, feeding, raising, and breeding of cattle were, at one time, some of the most popular tax shelters. Through deductions for prepaid feed and supplies, and in the case of breeding, through depreciation deductions for breeder animals, investors were able to shelter their income from other sources.

Economically, from an investor's standpoint, cattle feeding is essentially buying a commodity (beef), stuffing it with another commodity (grain), and hoping that the current cost of the grain commodity will work out to be less than the future cost of the beef commodity. Cattle feeding is a relatively short-term investment, since cattle are fed to boost their weight for slaughter for periods ranging from four months to one year. Cattle breeding, of course, is a longer-term venture and adds the element of possible gain from the sale of animals produced by the breeding herd as well as the breeding animals themselves.

Ranching, in its wider aspect, combines cattle feeding and breeding with the addition of the potential appreciation in the value of land if the rancher owns the grazing land. Other livestock investments might include dairy cows or the breeding and racing of race horses.

Since the adoption of the farm syndicate rules previously noted in connection with farming, livestock investments cannot be conducted in limited partnership form as a tax shelter. Today, livestock and cattle investments that seek to benefit from any remaining favorable tax rules are generally offered to individual investors and conducted under some type of agency contract between the individual investors and the sponsors of the investments. Limited partnerships formed to invest in cattle or other livestock today must rely solely on their economic potential for profit to attract investors.

TIMBER

Timber operations have characteristics that are common to both farm and mineral operations. Unlike crops, however, timber does not replace itself quickly. Once trees are cut and the stand replanted, it takes years to produce another marketable "crop." Unlike minerals, such as oil and gas, timber does eventually replace itself. What's more, it is much easier to find and assess a timber "deposit" which, unlike a pool of oil, is located above the ground.

The replacement aspect of timber is most important from an investor's point of view. An investor who buys minerals such as oil and gas knows he will not have more of this asset simply by waiting. The timber owner, however, can watch his asset grow as nature takes its course and further gain is not totally dependent on price increases. The elimination of preferential tax treatment for capital gain realized from the sale of timber (as well as any other capital asset), however, eliminated the major tax incentive for investing in timber.

Limited partnerships are available that invest in timber land. Obviously, these investments are long-term investments and are subject to risks. Disease, pests, and fire can undo the work of years. Timber prices do fluctuate, and return to investors may be delayed if cutting mature trees must be delayed because timber prices are depressed.

RESEARCH AND DEVELOPMENT

A typical research and development (R&D) investment involves an inventor or corporation that wants to develop a patentable idea. The corporation transfers the rights for the idea to a partnership in return for a general partner's interest. Investors are solicited to provide the necessary capital in return for limited partnership interests. The R&D work is then conducted by the partnership under contract with the corporation.

The limited partners, of course, bear the risk that the idea or product under development may not work out. If the project is a success, however, the limited partnership then owns the rights to the product, which can be sold to the corporation at a profit for the investors. Some corporations that have sponsored R&D partnerships have provided added inducement to investors in the form of stock rights or warrants.

The corporation using an R&D partnership to develop a successful product probably will pay more in royalties than it would have paid had it financed the R&D itself. The risk of failure, however, is shifted to the investors. What's more, no liabilities appear on the corporation's balance sheet because none are created. Also, in periods of high interest rates or tight money, financing for an R&D project may be difficult to obtain, and a limited partnership may be the most practical way to complete a project.

Although R&D partnerships were once a much sought-after investment, investor interest in these projects waned following the failure of several projects, notably those sponsored by Lear Aircraft (to develop a new type of airplane) and Storage Technology (to develop a new computer).

ENTERTAINMENT INDUSTRIES

Investors can participate in movie or film production under two basic arrangements: a *negative pickup arrangement* in which investors purchase a completed film or TV program; or a *production service arrangement* in which investors put up cash to actually produce a film or program. Of the two, the production service arrangement is the more common today. The negative pickup deals were more common in the heyday of tax shelters, but earned a bad reputation because many of them were sold at inflated prices with promised tax savings (which often failed to materialize) providing investors their only chance to profit.

In a production service arrangement, the investors are financing the actual production of a movie or TV film. Usually, the investors become limited partners in a production service company. At one time, the costs of production could be deducted for tax purposes when the costs were incurred. This permitted investor-partners in the production service company to deduct their share of the costs on their own tax returns to offset income from other sources. During this production stage, the service company would be earning no income, only incurring a loss, which flowed through to the partners. Now, investors must capitalize production costs and deduct them over the period income from the film is earned. This rule eliminated the tax shelter aspect of a production service arrangement.

After a film is complete, the distributor makes prints and distributes the film. Money from the distribution goes first to pay off any production loans and then to the production service partnership for distribution to the partners. Naturally, not every film is a success, and investors may end up with an economic loss. On a successful film, investors profit economically, but their return is no longer enhanced by the tax deferral that was available when production costs could be deducted as incurred.

How Limited Partnerships Have Changed to Reflect Current Conditions

As we have seen, most tax shelters took the form of limited partnerships because of the combination of the tax benefits of a partnership and limited liability for investors. As Congress has passed laws to curtail the effectiveness of tax shelters, the importance of tax shelter limited partnerships to investors has declined. This has not meant, however, that the limited partnership itself has declined as an attractive investment vehicle. The flexibility of this form of business organization permits investments to be structured to provide investors with the best possible return in the face of changing conditions.

The return from a limited partnership investment comes in three forms: cash flow, tax benefits, and appreciation. All successful limited partnership investments provide some combination of these three forms of investment return.

Cash flow is the actual after-tax cash distributed to or realized by the limited partner while he holds his interest and upon the liquidation of the partner's interest. Tax benefits are the tax savings generated by the underlying investment and passed through to the investor by the limited partnership. These tax benefits flow from initial deductions provided by many underlying investments and deductions generated over the life of the investment. Finally, appreciation is the actual rise in the value of an investment because values increase over time, such as has occurred with real estate; because of growth, such as the increase in the value of a stand of timber; or because of the actual activity of the limited partnership, such as the discovery of oil in an oil and gas limited partnership.

Although all limited partnership investments produce some combination of cash flow, tax benefits, and appreciation, they may not do so equally. The three forms of return are interrelated, so that an increase in one form of return is usually achieved to the detriment of the other two. For example, the tax benefits (deductions) from an investment may be increased through leverage (borrowing) or a higher purchase price. To the extent tax benefits are increased through borrowing, cash flow from the investment is reduced. More borrowing means higher payments of both principal and interest on the debt. Cash that would otherwise flow to the limited partners must be diverted to service the debt. To the extent tax benefits are increased through a higher purchase price, there is obviously less potential for appreciation.

Similarly, cash flow from an investment can be increased by reduced borrowing or reduced equity buildup in an investment. To the extent cash flow is increased by reduced borrowing, tax benefits are reduced. The lower debt service means lower deductions for interest payments and smaller "paper loss" deductions. To the extent cash flow is increased by reducing equity buildup, that is, by drawing out cash that would otherwise be working in the investment, the ultimate value of the investment is reduced. Finally, appreciation, or the buildup in value of a limited partnership investment, may be increased by sacrificing early tax benefits or by drawing less cash out during the course of an investment.

Essentially, the structure and type of a limited partnership investment determines the nature of the return to the investor. Accordingly, limited partnerships may be structured to yield greater cash flow with reduced tax benefits and appreciation; greater tax benefits with reduced cash flow and appreciation; or greater appreciation potential with reduced cash flow and tax benefits.

If a limited partnership is to attract investors, its structure must be responsive to investors' needs and the tax and economic conditions existing at the time. The shift from a high tax rate, high inflation environment to a lower tax rate, lower inflation environment saw a corresponding shift in the structure of limited partnership investments. Instead of structuring investments for maximum tax benefits through artificial or paper losses created by large borrowing, sponsors shifted to investments with reduced borrowing that offer less in the way of tax benefits and appreciation potential, but much more in the way of immediate tax sheltered cash flow.

CHAPTER **3**

What You Should Know About
Legal Organization and Structure

The partnership is an ancient form of business organization. You could probably trace its roots back to that time when the first two ancestors of modern man decided to cooperate on a hunt and share the results of their efforts. The more recent legal rules governing partnerships, along with the rest of the English common law, came with the colonists who settled along the Atlantic coast. Out of this early common law grew the state laws of 49 of our 50 states, and the confusion that results when there are possibly 50 different sets of rules governing the same type of transaction. To make state partnership laws uniform, the separate state legislatures (with the exception of Louisiana) adopted a uniform set of laws governing partnerships that is known, aptly enough, as the Uniform Partnership Act. In many particulars, the Uniform Partnership Act is a codification of partnership law as developed at common law.

Under common law, however, there was no such thing as a limited partnership. Partnerships were essentially viewed as an aggregate or collection of individuals engaged in the same business. As individuals, or proprietors of the business, partners were liable for all debts and obligations of the partnership just as if they were in business for themselves with no partners. To create limited partnerships required special legislation by the states. Again, to make limited partnership rules uniform, all states (except Louisiana) adopted the Uniform Limited Partnership Act in the form originally put forth in 1916.

In 1976, the National Conference of Commissioners on Uniform State Laws adopted a revision of the Uniform Limited Partnership Act. Since then, many states have enacted this later version. The key point, however, is that the limited partnership is a creature of state statute, and the purpose of the state statutes authorizing limited partnerships is to permit an investor to make an investment in partnership form without subjecting more than his investment to risk of loss. To receive the benefit of the statute, of course, the partners and the limited partnership must substantially comply with the provisions of the statute as enacted within the state in which the partnership is organized.

As a general matter, limited partnerships are permitted to engage in the same businesses as general partnerships. Both the Uniform Limited Partnership Act and the Revised Uniform Limited Partnership Act, however, permit the various states to deny specifically the privilege of operating as a limited partnership to certain types of business. In states that have elected to enact exceptions, banking and insurance are the most common businesses that are denied the right to operate as limited partnerships.

Formation of a Limited Partnership

The formation of a limited partnership generally requires the filing of a *certificate of limited partnership* by the partners. In addition to the certificate, two other documents are important to investors on the formation of a limited partnership. These are the *agreement of limited partnership* and the *limited partnership subscription agreement*. Each of these is discussed in turn, below.

A partnership that has at least one general partner and one limited partner, and that properly files a certificate and otherwise substantially complies with the applicable state limited partnership law, provides the limited partner with the protection of limited liability as to the obligations of the partnership. Notice that a limited partnership requires both general and limited partners. A limited partnership cannot consist of only limited partners. There must be at least one partner responsible for running the affairs of the partnership and fully responsible for the obligations of the partnership. This is unlike a corporation in which all shareholders enjoy the limited liability of their shareholder status.

While a limited partnership does require at least one general partner, in most states that general partner may be a corporation. In effect, using a corporate general partner protects the shareholders of the corporation from the unlimited liability of a general partner, even though the corporation, to the full extent of its assets, is exposed to general liability for partnership obligations. If the limited partners control the corporation serving as the general partner in a limited partnership, however, the limited partners may not receive the protection of limited partners. In this case, use of the corporation by the limited partners may be viewed as an attempt to evade the limited partnership requirements.

Use of a corporate general partner in a limited partnership also has tax ramifications. Recall that it is the IRS that determines limited partnership status for federal tax purposes. Unless the corporation meets certain requirements as to net worth and other factors, the IRS may view use of a corporate general partner as a means of giving the partnership the corporate characteristic of limited liability. This, in turn, may result in classification of the partnership for tax purposes as an association taxable as a corporation.

Generally, any individual, partnership, association, or corporation may become a limited partner in a limited partnership, although there may be exceptions in some states. Individuals who have not reached the age of majority may be general or limited partners in some states, even though all states limit the extent to which a minor may be held to contracts. Accordingly, a minor may be able to void a limited partnership agreement or subscription agreement to which he becomes a party, but may be able to hold a limited partnership interest received as a gift or under the Uniform Gift to Minors Act. An investor who desires to make a gift of a limited partnership interest to a child should, first, determine that there are no restrictions on the transfer in the partnership agreement, and second, explore with local counsel the best means to accomplish the transfer if it is permitted.

CERTIFICATE OF LIMITED PARTNERSHIP

A partnership cannot acquire the status of a limited partnership unless the partners sign and file with the proper state authorities a certificate of limited partnership. Filing this certificate is closely akin to the filing of articles of incorporation by a corporation. The primary purpose of the certificate is not to protect limited partners or investors, but to protect potential creditors of the partnership by informing them of the business and financial status of the partnership organization. Some states supplement the filing requirement by also requiring that a public notice of the certificate or the substance of the certificate be published in specified publications.

The reason for filing and public notice becomes obvious when you consider that creditors cannot look to limited partners for payment of partnership obligations and must be informed of the nature of the partnership. By the same token, if no certificate is filed, or a certificate is improperly filed, limited partners should not expect the protection of limited liability since potential creditors would not have been informed of their limited liability status.

In a public limited partnership with possibly hundreds or thousands of limited partners, filing a certificate of limited partnership that is signed by each limited partner could be quite an undertaking, a virtually impossible task for the partnership's sponsor or general partner. Many states recognize this and allow limited partners to execute the certificate by acknowledgment. Limited partners execute a power of attorney that gives the general partner the power to execute the certificate on their behalf. Such a power of attorney is usually included along with the limited partnership subscription agreement or other document signed when an investor acquires an interest in a limited partnership.

While the certificate of limited partnership is directed primarily to potential creditors of the partnership and the general public, it does contain a synopsis of the nature and character of the partnership and many of the rights and obligations of the limited partners. The following points generally must be covered in a certificate of limited partnership.

Basic Information. The certificate must contain the name of the partnership and the location of its principal place of business. It also must describe the nature of the partnership's business. A certificate of limited partnership, just as corporate articles, may be written with a very broad purpose clause. Typically, corporate articles may contain a phrase such as "and any other lawful business activity" within the description of the nature of the business to be carried on by the corporation. Such a broad purpose clause may not be desirable in a limited partnership when investors are seeking to invest only in a specified underlying activity. An investor in a real estate partnership may not be happy to find that he is suddenly in the oil and gas business. While rather farfetched, such is possible unless the business purpose of the partnership, as spelled out in the certificate and limited partnership agreement, is restricted to real estate.

Names of Partners. The names and addresses of each general and limited partner must be listed in the certificate of limited partnership. To protect the confidentiality of investors, some limited partnerships are organized in tiers so that other partnerships or nominees hold the limited partnership interests on behalf of investors.

Termination. The term or duration of the limited partnership is stated in the certificate. This is usually in the form of a specific date with a list of possible events or contingencies that would cause the partnership to terminate before the specified date.

Contributions. The certificate must list the amount of cash and/or the value of any other property contributed to the limited partnership by each limited partner. In addition to initial contributions, the certificate must state whether limited partners may be required to make additional contributions in the future and the conditions that will trigger the additional contributions. If a partner's initial contribution is to be paid into the partnership in installments or if additional contributions may be required, the effect of a limited partner's failure to make the required contributions should be spelled out.

Return of Contributions. The certificate of limited partnership must disclose any agreement to return limited partners' contributions, including the times and circumstances under which the contributions may be returned and whether the limited partners have the right to demand property in lieu of cash in return for their contributions.

Profit and Loss Sharing. The share of each partner in the profits of the partnership in return for his contribution must be disclosed as well as any other compensation to the partners to be paid out of partnership income. How expenses and losses are to be allocated must also be disclosed if different from the sharing of profits.

New and Substitute Partners. If the partnership may admit additional new partners to the limited partnership, this must be disclosed. Also, if a partner has the right to transfer his interest to another, this right must be disclosed in the certificate of limited partnership, as well as the procedure the partner must follow to substitute another in his place.

Multiple General Partners. If the limited partnership has more than one general partner, any priorities among the general partners must be disclosed in the certificate. Also, the certificate must disclose the right of any remaining general partners to continue the partnership and/or substitute a new general partner on the withdrawal or disqualification of a general partner.

Amendment. If there is any change in any of the particulars required to be disclosed in the certificate of limited partnership, or if the certificate in any way does not accurately disclose the substance of the partnership agreement, the certificate must be amended. The limited partnership certificate is canceled when the partnership is dissolved following its termination as specified in the certificate or if the partnership no longer has limited partners.

AGREEMENT OF LIMITED PARTNERSHIP

As far as the investors or limited partners are concerned, the heart of a limited partnership is the agreement of limited partnership. As previously noted, outsiders (the creditors of the partnership and members of the general public) are the primary concern of the certificate of limited partnership. The certificate regulates the relationship between the limited partnership and outsiders.

It is the agreement, however, that controls the relationships among the limited and general partners within the partnership and spells out what the general partners are agreeing to do on behalf of the limited partners. In short, it is the legal contract between the members of the partnership. It is the document that stipulates the rights and obligations of the general and limited partners with respect to each other.

In most cases, the limited partnership agreement for a public limited partnership is a lengthy and involved document. Since it may contain any provision that is not contrary to law, it may contain any provision desired by the partners. As a practical matter, however, limited partners will not have a say in structuring the terms of the agreement in a public limited partnership. It is really a take-it-or-leave-it proposition. But because it does regulate the limited partners' and the general partners' rights and obligations, you should review it, or have a trusted advisor review it on your behalf, *before* you make any investment. In the absence of a provision in the partnership agreement, you and other limited partners have few rights (see the discussion of the rights and obligations of limited partners, which follows).

If the agreement of limited partnership contains all of the information required by the certificate of limited partnership, the agreement may be filed in place of a separate certificate to serve as the limited partnership certificate. In private placements (as distinguished from public partnerships), the parties often want to keep their business arrangements confidential, and are more likely to file an abbreviated certificate rather than the full partnership agreement. Since full public disclosure is a requirement for securities (including limited partnership interests) sold to the general public, this confidentiality consideration is not a factor in public limited partnerships.

LIMITED PARTNERSHIP SUBSCRIPTION AGREEMENT

The subscription agreement is the document that you sign when you agree to purchase an interest in a limited partnership. It provides you, the limited partner, with evidence of your purchase and interest in the limited partnership and obligates you to make the required capital contribution.

The subscription agreement also usually contains a statement that you are qualified to make the investment and that you have read the prospectus and are familiar with and can accept the risk inherent in the underlying activity of the limited partnership. If not a separate document, the subscription agreement also contains the grant of a power of attorney by the limited partner to permit the general partner to act on the limited partner's behalf in matters relating to the partnership, possibly including the execution and filing of the certificate of limited partnership.

Once you sign the subscription agreement, you become obligated to pay for whatever limited partnership interest you have agreed to purchase and become obligated by the terms and conditions of the limited partnership agreement. It is the last step you should take in committing yourself to a limited partnership investment–*after* you or a trusted advisor have reviewed the prospectus and/or other offering documents and the partnership agreement and have satisfied yourself that the offering is as represented and meets your investment needs and objectives.

Rights and Obligations of Limited Partners

As a practical matter, limited partners have few rights other than those spelled out in the partnership agreement. That is why that document is so important. As the legal contract regulating the business relationship among the partnership, general partners, and limited partners, it is the source of the most important rights that limited partners can enforce against the general partners and the partnership. Nevertheless, the law does provide limited partners with certain limited rights, but even these can be varied or altered by agreement in many cases.

BOOKS AND RECORDS

Limited partners have the same rights as general partners as to access to the business records and ledgers of the partnership. A limited partner may inspect and copy the books of the partnership, although this right to inspect and copy generally must be exercised at reasonable times and in a reasonable manner.

A limited partner is entitled to receive general information and reports from the partnership that provide complete and accurate details as to the affairs of the partnership. A formal account of partnership affairs can be demanded and legally enforced by limited partners, according to the Uniform Limited Partnership Act, "whenever circumstances render it just and reasonable."

INCOME AND PROFITS

Limited partners are entitled to their shares of the income and profits of the partnership and any other compensation which is spelled out in the partnership agreement. Those provisions of the partnership agreement that detail how income, profits, and proceeds from the sale of partnership property are to be divided are of critical importance to the limited partners, and are often some of the most complicated. The partnership agreement may give particular partners shares of certain items of income or loss that are greater or less than the shares under the general profit-sharing ratio of the partnership.

For example, a limited partnership agreement may draw a distinction among cash flow or income from operations, cash from the sale of partnership property or assets, and income or loss as reported for tax purposes. Different partners may then be given different allocations of each of these classes of items. Other common provisions that may be contained in a limited partnership agreement may give the limited partners a share of income that is higher until the limited partners have recovered their investment and then is reduced in order to increase the income flowing to the general partners once the limited partners have recovered their contributions. In some cases, limited partners may be given an annual guaranteed cash payment that provides a minimum return on their investment.

The differing allocations of income or cash flow items may not just distinguish between limited and general partners. A limited partnership agreement may provide for different classes of limited partners, similar to different classes of stockholders that may be provided by a corporation's charter or articles. In the absence of an agreement to create different classes of limited partners which is reflected in the certificate of limited partnership, however, all limited partners stand on equal footing with respect to income allocations.

Unless actual distributions of income at specified times are required by the partnership agreement, there is nothing that forces the general partners to actually make distributions of cash. General partners, in the management of the affairs of the limited partnership, may retain cash for use by the partnership. A partnership that is earning income but not making distributions can create a real problem for limited partners. As we shall see in the next chapter, limited partners must pay taxes on their shares of partnership income whether or not that income is actually distributed. For this reason, investors may want to assure themselves that a limited partnership agreement specifies that at least a minimum distribution, sufficient to pay taxes, will be made whenever the partnership earns income that may create a tax liability for the partners.

RETURN OF CONTRIBUTION

A limited partner does have a limited right to a return of his capital contribution if the assets of the partnership exceed the liabilities of the partnership. This right, however, is carefully circumscibed and a limited partner may demand a return of his contribution, provided partnership assets are sufficient, only at the following times:

1. When all members of the partnership consent to the return of the limited partner's contributions.
2. When the limited partnership is dissolved.
3. On the date specified in the certificate of limited partnership for the return of contributions.

Limited partners have the right to demand only cash in return for their contribution, regardless of the type of property originally contributed, unless the certificate provides for return of contributions in some other form.

If no time is specified in the certificate of limited partnership for either the dissolution of the partnership or the return of partners' contributions, a limited partner may demand a return of his contribution at any time, provided he gives six months' notice in writing to all other members of the partnership. Needless to say, sponsors of limited partnerships always are sure to include a date for the dissolution of the partnership in the certificate of limited partnership to forestall demands by investors for a return of their investments on six months' notice.

COMPETITION

A limited partner generally may engage in a business in competition with the limited partnership in which he is a partner, although such competition may be prohibited by the partnership agreement. The rule is the other way around, however, for general partners. A general partner may not compete with the business of the partnership unless he is permitted to do so by the partnership agreement.

In many cases, general partners of public partnerships serve as general partners in more than one partnership. Accordingly, limited partnership agreements usually grant the general partner the right to compete and conduct other related businesses or activities, whether in partnership form or otherwise. You, as a limited partner, may want to ascertain for yourself that a general partner's other activities do not create too great a conflict of interest that can detract from the performance of the limited partnership in which you are investing.

NATURE OF THE PARTNERSHIP INTEREST

A limited partner must distinguish between his interest in the partnership and the partnership's interest in the assets of the partnership. Regardless of the underlying investments or activities of the limited partnership, the limited partner's interest in the partnership is considered to be personal property. As such, a limited partner may assign his interest to others and the interest is subject to the claims of the limited partner's creditors. The limited partner does not have a property interest in the underlying assets of the partnership, and creditors of the limited partner cannot reach the assets of the partnership.

While a limited partnership interest, as personal property, is assignable, an assignment of a limited interest by a limited partner does not make the assignee a limited partner. Only by meeting the conditions spelled out in the certificate of limited partnership for admitting new or substitute partners (if permitted), and by amending the certificate, can the recipient of an assignment of a limited partnership interest become a limited partner. For practical purposes, the distinction between a substitute limited partner and the assignee of a limited partnership interest may not be that important. The assignee of the interest is entitled to all economic benefits flowing from the interest, even though he is not obligated under the partnership agreement (the original limited partner remains obligated under the agreement following the mere assignment of his interest to another).

If a limited partner dies, his estate becomes responsible for any remaining obligations the limited partner had to the partnership at the time of his death. The executor or administrator of the limited partner's estate remains in possession of the rights the limited partner had in the partnership at the time of his death for the purpose of settling the estate.

ENFORCEMENT OF RIGHTS

A limited partner may enforce his rights as a limited partner, depending on the circumstances, by either seeking dissolution of the partnership or through a class or derivative action on behalf of the partnership against the general partners. In the event of fraud on the part of a general partner or a breach of the partnership agreement by a general partner, a limited partner has the same rights as a general partner in a general partnership to seek the judicially ordered dissolution of the partnership and the distribution of its assets.

Dissolution may also be sought when a limited partner has the right to a return of his contribution and the partnership refuses to return the contribution, or its assets are not sufficient to cover the liabilities owed to creditors of the partnership and the amount of the limited partner's contribution.

In many states, limited partners have rights similar to shareholders of a corporation to bring a class action on behalf of all limited partners or a derivative action on behalf of the partnership. These actions would be against the general partners for damages in the event the general partners breached their fiduciary responsibilities to the limited partners and/or the partnership. New York and Delaware are two of the states that specifically permit derivative actions on behalf of the limited partnership entity.

As a practical matter, limited partners in public partnerships may have little recourse against general partners other than through class or derivative actions in which the ultimate cost of the suit is, in effect, shared by all limited partners. The cost to a lone limited partner bringing a suit for dissolution may outweigh any benefit that partner could expect from a successful suit.

If the matter in dispute involves a securities law violation, keep in mind that class, derivative, or individual actions may be permitted under federal securities laws, as discussed further in Chapter 5.

OBLIGATIONS

A limited partner's obligations to a limited partnership are those primarily concerned with the capital contribution the limited partner agrees to make in return for his partnership interest. Once an investor agrees to become a limited partner by signing the subscription agreement, the investor becomes liable for the amount he agrees to pay to the partnership and remains liable for any unpaid portion of this amount as long as it remains unpaid. This obligation to pay the agreed-to capital contribution may be enforced by the partnership and, in some states, by creditors of the partnership.

If a limited partner receives any money or property from the partnership as a result of his capital contribution, the limited partner is liable to the partnership and holds the money or property in trust for the partnership to the extent the money or property is paid to him wrongfully or by mistake.

The liability of a limited partner to the extent of his agreed-to capital contribution is broader than it may appear on the surface. This liability continues even after the limited partner receives a return of his contribution if the capital is needed to satisfy partnership obligations to creditors who extended credit to the partnership before the limited partner received the return of capital. What's more, if any amount of a limited partner's agreed-to contribution remains unpaid and is forgiven or otherwise compromised by consent of the partners, the limited partner remains potentially liable to creditors who extended credit prior to the reduction to the full extent of the originally agreed-to contribution.

Rights and Obligations of General Partners

While general partners stand in a fiduciary relationship to the limited partners and the partnership and must conduct themselves accordingly, they nevertheless possess almost absolute control over the affairs of the partnership. This point must be clearly understood by investors before making an investment in a limited partnership.

The limited partnership has no equivalent to the "corporate democracy" that exists in a corporation. General partners, unlike corporate officers and directors, are not elected to their position and remain in power unless a court intervenes at the behest of limited partners for breaches of fiduciary duty. General poor management is not grounds for dissolution of a limited partnership or removal of a general partner.

Nevertheless, the power of a general partner in a limited partnership is subject to some limitations even though it does approach absolute power. The key idea is simply that a general partner may do anything that is not detrimental to the business of the partnership or contravenes the certificate or agreement of limited partnership. Generally, a general partner may not do any of the following without the consent or ratification of all limited partners.

1. Any act that runs against the certificate of limited partnership.
2. Sell, assign, or use for nonpartnership purposes any property of the partnership (except to the extent the sale or assignment is part of the partnership business).
3. Admit a new general partner to the partnership.
4. Admit a new limited partner to the partnership (unless permitted by the certificate of limited partnership).
5. Continue the partnership beyond the death, retirement, or other disqualification of another general partner (unless authorized by the certificate of limited partnership).
6. Any act that prevents the conduct of the ordinary business or activity of the partnership.
7. Confess a judgment against the partnership.

Outsiders to the partnership can assume that a general partner is acting for all general partners and for the partnership when he conducts partnership business. This means that any one general partner can obligate all general partners and the partnership, and all general partners are jointly and severally liable to third parties for the business acts of any general partner. General partners are also jointly and severally liable to third parties for the acts of agents and employees of the partnership. In short, principles of agency apply to the acts of general partners and they can bind the limited partnership by acts done within the scope of their actual or apparent authority.

Dissolution

As previously mentioned, most limited partnerships provide for dissolution upon a certain date or upon the happening of some earlier specified contingencies. Other than as called for in the certificate of limited partnership, a limited partnership may be dissolved by a limited partner in the enforcement of the limited partner's rights, as spelled out previously in the discussion of limited partners' rights.

A limited partnership also dissolves if a general partner dies, retires, or is otherwise disqualified from serving as a general partner unless provision is made in the partnership agreement for continuance by remaining general partners or a substitute general partner is agreed to by all limited partners. A sale of all partnership assets also may dissolve the partnership, unless provision is made for continuance in the partnership agreement.

A limited partnership agreement may provide that a vote by a specified percentage of limited partners can dissolve the partnership, although such a provision is unusual.

SETTLEMENT OF ACCOUNTS

On the dissolution of a limited partnership, claims to the assets of the partnership are handled in the following order of priority.

1. Claims of creditors are paid first. If a limited partner is also a creditor of the limited partnership, the limited partner would take priority along with other creditors to the extent of the credit extended to the partnership, but not for contributions.
2. After creditors, distributions are made to limited partners in the following order:
   (a) profits of the partnership to which the limited partners are entitled, and
   (b) capital contributed to the partnership by the limited partners.
3. Finally, after creditors and limited partners, general partners are entitled to any remaining assets in the following order:
   (a) for any amounts other than profits or capital contributions,
   (b) profits of the partnership to which the general partners are entitled, and
   (c) capital contributed to the partnership by the general partners.

Note that the priority of distribution between the limited and general partners can be varied by agreement. The most common variation is agreement to permit general partners to recover loans made to the partnership to cover operating deficits before any distributions are made to the limited partners.

If the assets of the partnership are not sufficient to cover in full the profits and contributions of the limited partners to which they are entitled on dissolution, the limited partners share in what is available in proportion to each of their contributions and claims to partnership income.

CHAPTER **4**

What You Should Know About Partnership Taxation

The subject of the taxation of partners and partnerships was briefly introduced in the introductory chapter. Recall that the key feature of a partnership for federal income tax purposes is that it is not, in the usual case, a taxpaying entity. Rather, the nature of a partnership for tax purposes is one of a conduit through which tax consequences flow to the individual partners, and this is true regardless of whether the partnership in question is a general partnership or a limited partnership. It is around this core concept that the partnership tax rules are built.

The part of the Internal Revenue Code spelling out the partnership tax rules, like many other parts of the law, can be confusing and, at times, inexplicable, especially to the uninitiated. Rest assured that we are not about to explore partnership tax rules in all their glorious complication. Our goal is to cover, in as uncomplicated a way as possible, those areas of most concern to you as an investor, or potential investor, in a public limited partnership.

Tax Basis, the Beginning and End

Perhaps the most logical starting place is with the investment made to acquire a partnership interest. This investment gives the partner his first important number, his "cost" or "tax basis." Every limited partner must know the tax basis of his partnership interest for several very important reasons.

1. The basis is used to figure the amount of taxable gain or loss a partner realizes on the sale of his interest.
2. The basis at the time a partnership or a partner's interest in a partnership is liquidated determines the tax consequences of the liquidation.
3. The basis on the last day of the year establishes the primary limit on the amount of a partner's share of partnership losses that the partner can take as a tax deduction.
4. The basis establishes the amount of the distributions from a partnership which a partner can receive without taxes in addition to those that arise on the flow-through of partnership taxable income.

The starting point for determining a partner's tax basis is the amount of cash (or other property) contributed to the partnership in exchange for the partnership interest. This is essentially the same rule that applies to other investments. For example, if an investor pays $5,000 for 100 shares of stock, that investor's tax basis is $5,000 and his gain or loss on a later sale of the 100 shares of stock will be determined by how much more or less than the $5,000 the investor receives. In the usual case, the stockholder's $5,000 basis will not change as long as he holds the stock. This is not the case, however, for a partnership interest.

The original tax basis of a partner in his partnership interest must be adjusted to reflect events occurring after the purchase of the partnership interest. These adjustments are necessary to preserve the conduit nature of the partnership. The original basis established by a contribution to a partnership (the purchase price of the interest) is increased by the partner's share of taxable income and tax-exempt income of the partnership. The original basis is decreased by the partner's share of partnership distributions, partnership losses, partnership expenditures that are not deductible in computing taxable income or loss and that are not capital expenditures, and the depletion deduction for oil and gas wells.

Any liabilities or debt incurred by a partnership also may affect a partner's tax basis. Each partner's share of a partnership liability is treated as money contributed and increases the partner's basis. However, since a limited partner cannot be held responsible for partnership debts beyond his capital contribution, partnership debt generally does not affect a limited partner's tax basis. The one exception to this rule is for nonrecourse liabilities for which no partner, including the general partner, is personally liable. If a limited partnership incurs a nonrecourse liability for which no partner can be held personally liable, then all partners, including limited partners, have their tax bases increased by a proportionate part of the nonrecourse liability. A decrease in partnership liabilities causes a corresponding decrease in the tax bases of those partners whose bases were increased by the liabilities when they arose.

TAX BASIS AND DISTRIBUTIONS

As noted above, the reason for the adjustments to a partner's tax basis for his partnership interest is to preserve the conduit nature of the partnership for tax purposes. A partner is taxed on his share of partnership income whether or not that income is distributed. If a partnership realizes income and does not immediately distribute that income to the partners, the partners, nevertheless, pay tax just as if the income had been distributed. If the partners were subject to tax on a later actual distribution of the income that had already been taxed, the partners, in effect, would be subjected to a double tax on the same income. A simple example will illustrate this important concept.

EXAMPLE. A limited partner in the XYZ Limited Partnership acquired his partnership interest for $5,000 in 1988. This amount is the limited partner's original cost basis or tax basis for his partnership interest. There were no other activities in 1988 that would affect this partner's tax basis.

In 1989, the XYZ Limited Partnership earns income from its activities and our limited partner's share of that income is $400. XYZ makes no distributions of income in 1989. Our limited partner, however, must report his $400 share of partnership income for 1989, just as if he had earned that income directly. The limited partner's share of partnership income also increases his tax basis in his partnership interest from $5,000 to $5,400. There are no other activities that affect our limited partner's tax basis during 1989, so the limited partner's tax basis stands at $5,400 at the beginning of 1990.

During 1990, XYZ earns no income but distributes $400 to our limited partner. There are no other events during 1990 that would affect our limited partner's basis. As a result of this distribution, the limited partner realizes no taxable income. Rather, the amount of the distribution reduces the limited partner's tax basis from $5,400 back to $5,000, and this is the limited partner's basis for his partnership interest at the beginning of 1991.

Through the mechanism of the basis adjustment, the conduit nature of the partnership is preserved, and the limited partner in our example pays tax only once on his $400 share of partnership income. Only if a distribution exceeds a partner's tax basis is the distribution subject to tax, and then only to the extent of the amount in excess of basis. If, in the previous example, XYZ were liquidated in 1991 and distributed $5,000 to the limited partner, the $5,000 would simply be a recovery of basis and there would be no tax on the limited partner. The distribution would reduce the limited partner's basis from $5,000 to zero.

CHARACTER OF GAIN OR LOSS

The tax basis of a partnership interest also determines the amount of gain or loss a partner realizes on the sale or other disposition of the interest. For instance, if a limited partner has a tax basis of $5,000 for his interest in a limited partnership and sells that interest for $6,000, the partner realizes a gain of $1,000. Again, this is similar to the rule that applies to most other investments. For instance, a shareholder with a $5,000 basis for corporate stock who sells that stock for $6,000 also realizes a $1,000 gain. For the shareholder, the gain is a capital gain. For the partner, however, the gain may or not be a capital gain. Again, the tax law attempts to preserve the conduit nature of the partnership on a sale or other disposition of a partnership interest.

Let's back up a minute and analyze why a partner might be able to sell a partnership interest with a basis to the partner of $5,000 to another investor for $6,000. First, there could be unrealized capital appreciation in the assets held by the partnership. For instance, suppose a partner acquired a 1 percent partnership interest for $5,000 in a partnership that used the partners' capital contributions to acquire raw land for investment and the value of the land increased by 20 percent. Now the partner's share of that land would be worth $6,000 and, for the most part, so would the partner's interest in the partnership.

Suppose, however, that the partnership, instead of acquiring raw land, used the partners' capital contributions to acquire property that would be resold in the ordinary course of the partnership's business. Property acquired with a partner's $5,000 contribution could be resold for $6,000. The partner, in this case, would be unwilling to sell his 1 percent interest for $5,000, but would insist on $6,000, the amount he could realize by simply holding his partnership interest.

In the second situation presented, if the partner held his interest until the partnership sold the property for $6,000, the partner would have to report his $1,000 share of partnership income from the sale of the property. This income would be ordinary income since it arises from the sale of property in the ordinary course of business, in other words, from the sale of inventory. The partner cannot avoid this ordinary income characterization by selling his partnership interest before the ordinary income is realized by the partnership. A sale by the partner of his partnership interest with a basis of $5,000 for $6,000 when that $1,000 difference represents unrealized appreciation in ordinary income assets is treated as ordinary income and not capital gain.

In the jargon of the tax law, assets that would produce ordinary income to the partnership and that result in ordinary income to a partner who sells his partnership interest before the realization of that income by the partnership are termed "unrealized receivables and substantially appreciated inventory." In effect, these terms encompasses every asset that would produce ordinary income at the partnership level, including ordinary income that would arise from the various "recapture" provisions contained in the Internal Revenue Code. In short, a partner who would realize ordinary income from a partnership cannot convert that ordinary income into capital gain by selling his partnership interest before the income is realized by the partnership.

To sum up the characterization of gain or loss on the sale or disposition of a partnership interest then, gain or loss is generally characterized as a capital gain or loss to the extent of the difference between the amount realized for the partnership interest and the partner's tax basis for the interest at the time of sale. However, to the extent any gain realized by the selling partner is attributable to unrealized receivables or substantially appreciated inventory items of the partnership, gain is characterized as ordinary income.

Although the various partnership rules on basis adjustment, distributions, and income characterization are quite complex (we have only scratched the surface), the key point for an investor in a public limited partnership is that they are all designed to preserve the conduit nature of the partnership for tax purposes. A public limited partnership will supply investors with all necessary numbers through its annual tax report to partners (Schedule K-1, Form 1041). You, as an investor, however, must be aware of the significance of these numbers and how they affect your overall tax liability.

Income and Loss of a Partnership

Although a partnership generally is not a taxable entity, a partnership generally computes its taxable income just like an individual, but the tax consequences are passed through to the partners. What's more, the pass-through or conduit is not simply for income or loss. Rather, each item that enters into the computation of taxable income is taken into account separately by the partners. The partners treat each item as if they received their share directly from the source of the item to the partnership.

For example, if a limited partnership realizes a $100,000 capital gain, a 1-percent limited partner would report $1,000 of capital gain income. If the partnership received $100,000 in dividends, a 1-percent partner would report receipt of $1,000 of dividend income. The same is true for everything—every item of income, loss, or deduction or tax credit— that can have an effect on a partner's individual tax return.

SPECIAL ALLOCATIONS OF INCOME OR LOSS

As noted in connection with the discussion of the partnership agreement in Chapter 3, that agreement may give particular partners or classes of partners shares of certain items of income or loss that are greater or less than the shares under the general profit sharing ratio of the partnership. For example, the partnership agreement may provide that limited partners are entitled to 100 percent of deductions for depreciation generated by the partnership's activities even though limited partners, as a group, are entitled to only an 80 percent share of all partnership profits and losses (with the remaining 20 percent going to the general partners). The allocation of specific income, loss, deduction, or tax credit items in a ratio that does not conform to the general profit-and-loss sharing ratio is called a "special allocation."

In order for a special allocation to be given effect for tax purposes, the special allocation must also have a "substantial economic effect." If a special allocation lacks this substantial economic effect, the Internal Revenue Service will ignore it and make the allocation of items for tax purposes conform to the normal profit-and-loss allocation of the partnership.

In the most simple terms, a special allocation has substantial economic effect when the allocation, in addition to the tax consequences, affects the capital accounts of the partners. A partner's capital account measures the partner's investment in the partnership, that is, what that partner would receive at any given moment if the partnership were liquidated. If capital accounts are adjusted for special allocations, and partnership assets must be distributed according to capital accounts, then the special allocations must actually affect the partners' shares of the economic income or loss of the partnership. This is essentially the position of the Internal Revenue Service in a quite lengthy set of income tax regulations dealing with special allocations in partnership agreements.

In the situation set out previously in which limited partners receive 100 percent of depreciation deductions but only 80 percent of income, the special allocation of depreciation would not be honored for tax purposes unless the depreciation allocated to limited partners also reduced their capital accounts by the full amount of the depreciation. In other words, the limited partners would have to bear any economic loss up to the full amount of depreciation in order for the full amount of depreciation to be available to reduce the taxable incomes of the limited partners.

RETROACTIVE ALLOCATIONS

At one time, investors were solicited near year's end for limited partnership investments. In the case of tax shelter partnerships, an investor could buy a full year's worth of tax losses through a year-end investment, if the partnership provided for retroactive allocations of income or loss. When the goal of the partnership was not primarily tax shelter, a retroactive allocation could entice reluctant investors with a full year's share of partnership income or cash flow for a year-end investment. The partnership agreement would provide an allocation of a full year's share of income or loss to any partner acquiring an interest by the end of the year.

Under the tax law now, a new partner can receive no share of any income, gain, loss, deduction, or credit realized or sustained by the partnership before the partner entered the partnership and have that allocation recognized for tax purposes. Also, to prevent avoidance of this rule by partnerships that make cash payments for deductible items late in the year, payments made by a cash-method partnership which apply to items accrued earlier in the year must be assigned to each day in the period to which they relate and allocated among the partners in proportion to their interests in the partnership on each day.

The practical effect of the retroactive allocation rules is that investors in limited partnerships that have already begun operations receive only a share of partnership items for their first year of investment in proportion to their time as limited partners compared to the time the partnership has been operating during that year. For example, if a calendar-year partnership begins operation on June 1, a partner acquiring an interest on August 1 is entitled to 5/7ths of his normal share of any partnership items generated during the partnership's year ending on December 31.

GUARANTEED ALLOCATIONS FOR CAPITAL

In some limited partnerships, the investor-limited partners, or a class of limited partners, may be guaranteed a minimum return based on the amount of their initial capital contributions regardless of the income of the partnership. These guaranteed payments which are made without regard to partnership income are ordinary income to the recipient partners and, if otherwise deductible, are deductible in computing a partnership's taxable income. In effect, guaranteed payments for the use of partners' capital are in the nature of interest and are treated as such for tax purposes.

A similar rule applies to guaranteed payments to partners in exchange for services. Such guaranteed payments for services are more likely to be made to general, rather than limited, partners. Guaranteed payments in exchange for services are in the nature of wages or salary and are treated as such for federal income tax purposes.

ORGANIZATION AND SYNDICATION COSTS

The costs of organizing and syndicating a limited partnership are not immediately deductible in computing the taxable income of the partnership. The actual costs of organizing a limited partnership must be charged to a capital account and then deducted over a period of at least sixty months.

The costs of syndicating a limited partnership are not deductible at all. Syndication costs are, generally, all the expenses involved in selling partnership interests to investors. They include the following:

1. Brokerage fees.
2. Registration fees.
3. Legal fees of the underwriter or placement agent and the issuer for securities advice and tax advice pertaining to the adequacy of tax disclosures in the prospectus or placement memorandum.
4. Accounting fees for the preparation of representations included in the offering materials.
5. Printing costs of the prospectus, placement memorandum, and any other material for promoting and selling partnership interests.

At one time, some partnerships attempted to get around the rules barring deductions for syndication costs and requiring capitalization of organization costs by allocating partnership income to the general partner. Instead of providing a reimbursement to the general partner for these expenses out of invested funds, the partnership agreement would allocate a share of partnership income to the general partner. The effect for the investors was equivalent to a deduction, since partnership income allocated to the investors would be reduced by the income allocated to the general partner.

Now, however, the Internal Revenue Service may treat allocations of partnership income made for property or services provided to the partnership as payments by the partnership for the property or services. This power goes beyond allocations of income in lieu of payments for organization and syndication costs, and extends to all income allocations for property or services, whatever their nature.

Restrictions on Partnership-Generated Tax Losses

While the government is more than willing to allow investors in limited partnerships to report and pay taxes on as much income from their investments as possible, it is somewhat stingy in allowing investor use of deductions or losses generated by limited partnerships. The use of tax deductions or losses flowing through the conduit of a limited partnership may be restricted or limited by three different tax rules. The following provides a brief, "get acquainted" view of these rules, and it is not meant to be a full and complete exposition of these provisions.

One of the limitations was mentioned briefly in connection with the role of a partner's basis in his partnership interest. A tax loss generated by a partnership is deductible by a partner only to the extent of the partner's tax basis for his partnership interest as of the end of the tax year in which the loss arose. A loss that exceeds basis may be deducted to the extent of the basis, and the excess loss may be carried over to future years and deducted against any future increase in basis. If there is an unused loss at the time a partner disposes of his partnership interest through a sale, exchange, or liquidation, the loss may be deducted at that time. The loss in this latter case generally is considered a capital loss.

In addition to the basis limitation on the use of losses or deductions generated by a limited partnership, there are two other rules that may come into play. In both cases, the rules are not directed solely to limited partnerships but apply generally to many investment activities. Limited partnerships, however, are often especially vulnerable to their application.

AT-RISK RULE

Congress enacted the "at-risk" provisions to curb what were perceived to be abuses in the use of nonrecourse financing. In a nonrecourse loan, the lender can look only to the financed asset for repayment. Before the at-risk rule was enacted, an investor could purchase an asset with nonrecourse financing, or through a limited partnership in which the investor was shielded from liability for partnership borrowings, and still take deductions based on the amount he put up in cash plus the amount of the debt (for which he had no real liability), that is, his tax basis.

Now, under the at-risk provisions, deductions from an activity may be taken to the extent of income from the activity. Income includes gain on sale of assets used in the activity as well as gain from a sale of the investment itself. In other words, to the extent an activity produces income, there is no at-risk limit on the deductions generated by that activity which may be used to offset that income.

In addition to deductions equal to income from an activity, an investor may take deductions in excess of income to the extent the investor is at risk. Amounts at risk in an activity include the amount of money invested, the adjusted basis of any property contributed to the activity, and borrowed amounts for which the borrower is personally liable for repayment or has pledged property other than the property in the activity to secure payment. The amount considered at risk for subsequent years is reduced by any allowable loss for the current year. Prior loss deductions are recaptured, that is, are reportable as income, if an amount formerly at risk in an activity becomes nonrecourse.

PASSIVE LOSS RULE

The Tax Reform Act of 1986 placed a major restriction on the use of certain types of investments as a means to defer tax on income from sources other than these investments. The passive loss rule essentially provides that losses from "passive activities" can be used only to offset income from passive activities. Similarly, a tax credit generated by a passive activity can be used only to offset tax liability attributable to a passive activity.

Generally speaking, a passive activity is any activity that involves the conduct of a trade or business in which the taxpayer does not materially participate. Also included are most activities involving the rental of real or personal property. Portfolio income, such as dividends, interest, and royalties, is not considered income from passive activities under the rule. Any loss or credit that cannot be used because of the rule may be carried over to future years and applied to passive income or tax liability attributable to passive income in subsequent years.

Pre-1987 Investments. The special limitation on losses and credits from passive activities generally applies to all tax years after 1986. However, for losses and credits generated by an investment made before October 22, 1986 (the date the Tax Reform Act of 1986 was enacted), the law provides a phase-in of the rule. Losses and credits from passive activities entered into before October 22, 1986, in excess of income and tax liability from passive activities, may be taken in the following percentages in the years indicated: 1987–65 percent; 1988–40 percent; 1989–20 percent; and 1990–10 percent.

Special Considerations for Limited Partners. In the case of a limited partnership interest, special considerations apply in the application of the passive loss rule. Since a limited partner generally is precluded from participating in the partnership's business if the partner is to retain limited liability status, material participation is not possible and a limited partnership interest is automatically passive. This means that income, deductions, and tax credits passed through to a limited partner generally are considered passive income, deductions, and credits, subject to these important exceptions:

1. Portfolio income (dividends, interest, etc.) earned by a limited partnership and passed through to the partners is not passive income under the passive loss rule. Rather, this income remains portfolio income to the limited partners.

2. The Internal Revenue Service has been given the power to issue regulations permitting or requiring income from certain limited partnership interests to be classified as passive income, portfolio income, or as income not arising from a passive activity. Exercise of this authority could affect the classification of income passed through to limited partners by a limited partnership.

3. The Revenue Act of 1987 provides special rules for "publicly traded partnerships." Net income from a publicly traded partnership that is not subject to corporate taxation is treated as portfolio income and net losses from a publicly traded partnership can be used only to offset future income from that partnership. These special rules for publicly traded partnerships are discussed further in the next section.

Publicly Traded Partnerships Treated As Corporations

As previously noted, a partnership generally is not subject to tax at the partnership level, but rather, income and loss of the partnership is subject to tax at the partner's level. A partner's share of partnership income generally is determined regardless of whether he receives any corresponding cash distributions. Similarly, partnership deductions, losses, and credits are taken into account at the partner level for tax purposes. By way of contrast, a corporation generally is subject to tax at the entity level, and distributions on corporate stock generally are subject to tax at the shareholder level.

As discussed in Chapter 2, the Internal Revenue Service makes the determination of whether an entity is a partnership for tax purposes based on corporate characteristics specified in the income tax regulations. If an entity is classified as a partnership, income and loss are subject to tax at the partner level rather than at the partnership level, regardless of the activities or method of operation of the partnership.

In response to the growing use of publicly traded partnerships (those that came to be known as master limited partnerships) to achieve the advantages of corporate-like operation and organization combined with partnership tax treatment, Congress decided to treat certain *publicly traded partnerships* as corporations for Federal income tax purposes. Note that this treatment applies to "publicly traded partnerships," as defined in the next section, and *not* to "public partnerships," that is, partnerships whose interests are simply offered for sale to the general public. What's more, this treatment does not apply to all publicly traded partnerships, and the important exceptions also are discussed in some detail in the next section.

WHAT IS A PUBLICLY TRADED PARTNERSHIP?

A publicly traded partnership is defined as a partnership in which the interests are:

1. Traded on an established securities market, or

2. Readily tradable on a secondary market or the substantial equivalent of a secondary market.

Established securities markets include any national securities exchange registered under the Securities Exchange Act of 1934 and any local or regional exchange. For example, the New York and American

Stock Exchanges and the Pacific Coast and Philadelphia-Baltimore-Washington Exchanges are established securities markets. In addition, an over-the-counter market that is characterized by an interdealer quotation system which regularly provides quotations by identified brokers or dealers is an established securities market. For example, the NASDAQ market is an established securities market.

Perhaps more difficult to get a handle on, and a provision which is likely to lead to substantial litigation, is the part of the definition that treats a partnership as publicly traded if interests are readily tradable on a secondary market or the substantial equivalent of a secondary market. The purpose of this part of the definition is to snare those partnerships that are not traded on an established securities market, but whose partners are readily able to buy, sell, or exchange their partnership interests in a manner that is comparable in an economic sense to trading on an established securities market.

According to the Conference Committee Report on the 1987 tax legislation which attempts to explain this legislation, a secondary market generally exists if there is a person standing ready to make a market in the interest. Also, a partnership interest is readily tradable if the interest is regularly quoted by persons such as brokers or dealers who are making a market in the interest. For instance, if a partnership interest is traded on a market essentially equivalent to an over-the-counter market, the partnership interest is publicly traded. (IRS has announced, however, that it will not consider a partnership to be publicly traded unless more than 5 percent of the interests in the partnership change hands during the year.)

If there is no identifiable market maker, but the holder of a partnership interest has a readily available, regular, and ongoing opportunity to sell or exchange his interest through a public means of obtaining or providing information of offers to buy or sell interests, the substantial equivalent of a secondary market exists. Also, the substantial equivalent of a secondary market exists if prospective buyers and sellers have the opportunity to buy or sell interests within time periods and with the regularity and continuity that a market maker would provide.

If the partnership provides a regular plan of redemptions or repurchases, or similar acquisitions of interests in the partnership so that holders of partnership interests have readily available, regular and on-going opportunities to dispose of their interests, the interests, most likely, would be considered readily tradable on the substantial equivalent of a secondary market.

While attempting to pin down from the Conference Committee Report exactly when a partnership interest will be considered readily tradable on a secondary market may be an exercise in futility, the report does provide specific situations in which partnership interests, although bought and sold, will not be considered readily tradable on a secondary market. The following situations, as gleaned from the Conference Committee Report, do *not* make a partnership publicly traded:

- Interests can be traded in a market that is publicly available, but offers to buy or sell interests normally are not accepted within time periods that are comparable to those in which offers are accepted in a secondary market.

- There are occasional accommodation trades of partnership interests, for instance, if the general partner or partnership sometimes purchases interests from other partners, but not as a result of a put or call right, or if the underwriter that handled the offering arranges such accommodation trades.

- The general partner provides information to its partners regarding their desire to buy or sell interests to each other, or arranges transfers between partners, but does not offer to buy or redeem interests or issue additional interests to such partners.

- Occasional and irregular repurchases or redemptions by the partnership, or acquisitions by the general partner, of interests in the partnership.

- Occasional actual transfers of interests or assignments of rights, if the partnership agreement provides that partnership interests may not be transferred and rights to income or other attributes may not be assigned, or if the partnership agreement provides that partners have only a restricted and limited right to transfer partnership interests or assign partnership income or other attributes. (This latter provision is designed to allow the partnership agreement to permit transfers on death or in the case of divorce, and to allow partners to make gifts of partnership interests to family members.)

- Partnership interests are not traded on an established securities market and the general partner and the partnership have the right to refuse to recognize trades in a secondary market and exercise the right by taking action so that trades or assignments are not recognized.

IMPORTANT EXCEPTIONS

While the tax law now treats many publicly traded partnerships as corporations, it makes some very important exceptions, primarily for partnerships engaged in real estate and natural resource (such as oil and gas) operations. Essentially, the exceptions are keyed to the type of income realized by a publicly traded partnership. A publicly traded partnership is not treated as a corporation, and partnership tax rules apply, if 90 percent or more of the partnership's gross income is "qualifying income." Qualifying income includes the following:

1. Interest, but this category does not include amounts contingent on profits or interest earned in pursuit of a financial or insurance business.

2. Dividends.

3. Rents from real property. Although amounts contingent on profits are excluded from this category, real property rents based on a fixed percentage of receipts or a fixed percentage of gross sales are included.

4. Gain from the disposition of real property. In the case of real property sold to customers in the ordinary course of business, gross income is not reduced by the inventory costs of property taken into account in determining gain from the sales.

5. Income and gains from natural resource activities. Specifically, natural resources include fertilizer, geothermal energy, and timber, as well as oil and gas and products of oil and gas.

6. Any gain from the disposition of a capital asset or asset held for the production of income that falls within categories (1) through (5) of the preceding.

7. Income and gains from commodities (other than those held for sale to customers in the ordinary course of business) or futures, options, or forward contracts on commodities (including foreign currency transactions of a commodity pool), but only if a principal activity of the partnership is the buying and selling of such commodities, futures, options, or forward contracts. This category of qualifying income excludes typical commodity pools from treatment as corporations.

Grandfather Rule for Partnerships Existing on December 17, 1987. In addition to the exceptions to the treatment of publicly traded partnerships as corporations in the case of partnerships with qualifying income, the tax law also makes an exception for partnerships that were in existence on December 17, 1987. Unlike the qualifying income rule, the exception for existing partnerships is only temporary. A publicly traded partnership that was in existence on December 17, 1987 will be treated as a corporation for taxable years beginning after December 31, 1997.

Partnerships covered by the ten-year grandfather rule include partnerships that filed registration statements with the SEC on or before December 17, 1987, that indicated that the partnership was to be a publicly traded partnership. Also included are partnerships that filed statements with state regulatory commissions on or before December 17, 1987, that sought permission to restructure a portion of a corporation as a publicly traded partnership whether or not the partnership was actually in existence on December 17, 1987.

EFFECT OF TREATING A PARTNERSHIP AS A CORPORATION

If a publicly traded partnership is treated as a corporation under the tax law as discussed, the partnership is treated as if it contributed all of its assets and liabilities to a newly formed corporation in exchange for all of the corporation's stock. The stock of the corporation is then treated as if it were distributed to the partners in complete liquidation of the partnership.

For the partners, the deemed incorporation followed by partnership liquidation may not have an immediate tax consequence. The incorporation is a tax-free transaction, and the liquidation of the partnership may be tax free. However, if the value of the deemed stock distributed to partners in liquidation of their partnership interests exceeds their bases in their partnership interests, taxable gain does result. This will be the case whenever the value of a partner's interest exceeds his tax basis for that interest at the time of the deemed incorporation and partnership liquidation.

More important to the partners is likely to be the effect on income earned by the partnership of treating the partnership as a corporation. First, the partnership becomes subject to the corporate tax on income earned by the partnership. This tax reduces the amount of income available for distribution to the partners. Second, income distributed to the partners then is subject to additional tax as a corporate dividend. In short, the tax benefits of partnership operation are lost, and income of the partnership is subjected to tax at both the entity and individual levels.

Publicly Traded Partnerships and the Passive Loss Rule

As discussed in connection with the restrictions on partnership-generated tax losses, deductions from passive trade or business activities, to the extent they exceed income from passive activities, generally may not be deducted against income from other sources. Similarly, credits from passive activities generally may be used only to offset tax attributable to passive activities. Suspended losses and credits may be carried forward and used against income or tax liability attributable to passive activities realized in future years.

Generally speaking, an interest in a limited partnership as a limited partner is considered a passive activity, although the Internal Revenue Service may issue regulations that could alter this result in certain cases. Publicly traded partnerships that are not treated as corporations because they have qualifying income or are subject to the ten-year grand-father rule, however, are subject to a special passive loss rule. Publicly traded partnerships, defined in the same way as under the provisions that treat certain publicly traded partnerships as corporations, do not produce passive income or losses that can be used to offset income from passive activities.

Income from publicly traded partnerships is not treated as passive income for purposes of the passive loss rule. Each partner in a publicly traded partnership treats a loss, if any, from the partnership as separate from income and loss from any other publicly traded partnership, and also as separate from income or loss from passive activities. Net income from publicly traded partnerships is treated as portfolio income under the passive loss rule.

A net loss attributable to an interest in a publicly traded partnership may not be deducted against the partner's other income, but must be suspended and carried forward. These net losses can be applied against net income from the partnership in future years. When a partner disposes of his entire interest in a publicly traded partnership, any remaining suspended losses may be deducted against other income at that time.

According to the Conference Committee Report on the 1987 tax legislation that enacted the special rules for publicly traded partnerships: the intended overall result of the special passive loss rule is that net losses and credits of a partner from each publicly traded partnership be suspended at the partner level; carried forward (but not back) and netted only against income from, or tax liability attributable to, that publicly traded partnership; and that suspended losses are allowed on the complete disposition of a partner's interest in a partnership.

Despite the special passive loss rule for publicly traded partnerships not treated as corporations, a partner in a publicly traded partnership that is engaged in the construction or rehabilitation of low-income housing may still be entitled to the special tax credits available for such activities. A partner in a publicly traded partnership may utilize his share of partnership low-income housing credits and rehabilitation credits against tax liability attributable to nonpartnership income to the extent of his unused $25,000 deduction-equivalent allowance. The $25,000 allowance of deduction-equivalent credits applies at the partner level, to the extent the amount of such credits exceeds the partner's regular tax liability attributable to income from the partnership. The credits are allowable under the partner's $25,000 allowance to the extent that the partner has not fully utilized the allowance with respect to losses and credits from passive activities otherwise allowed under the regular passive loss rule.

ILLUSTRATION OF PASSIVE LOSS RULE
FOR PUBLICLY TRADED PARTNERSHIPS

To help put the passive loss rule as applied to publicly traded partnerships in perspective, let's look at a relatively simple example. Let's assume an investor owns limited partnership interests in two limited partnerships, but otherwise engages in no other passive activities. Limited Partnership A is a publicly traded limited partnership, as previously defined, but it is not subject to being treated as a corporation because 90 percent of its gross income is from real estate activities. Limited Partnership B is not a publicly traded partnership, even though the investor acquired his interest in Partnership B as a result of a public offering.

For the current tax year, Limited Partnership A produced a net loss passed through to the investor in the amount of $1,000. Limited Partnership B, on the other hand, produced net income passed through to the investor in the amount of $1,500 (this income was not portfolio income to the partnership). Neither partnership produced income or loss for the investor in any previous tax year.

In this situation, the investor cannot use the $1,000 loss from Partnership A to offset his $1,500 of income from Partnership B. The investor must report his $1,500 of passive activity income from Limited Partnership B which is not publicly traded. The investor's loss from publicly traded Limited Partnership A is suspended, and the investor may carry this amount forward to offset income he may eventually realize from Limited Partnership A. If the loss is still unused when the investor disposes of his interest in Limited Partnership A, he may take a deduction for the unused loss at that time.

Now let's reverse the situation, that is, let's assume that Limited Partnership A, the publicly traded partnership, produces net income for the investor in the amount of $1,500 and that Limited Partnership B, the nonpublicly traded partnership, produces a net loss for the investor in the amount of $1,000. In this case, the investor cannot use the loss from Partnership B to offset the $1,500 of income from Partnership A. The $1,500 of income realized by the investor from Partnership A is treated as portfolio income under the passive loss rule. The $1,000 loss from Partnership B, however, is a passive loss under the passive loss rule. If the investor realized income from other passive sources, this loss could be used to offset that passive income. In the absence of income from passive sources, the $1,000 loss is suspended and carried over to future years under the regular passive loss rule, that is, it may be deducted against income realized in the future from any passive activity, not just Partnership B.

Let's try one more variation. Let's assume that neither Limited Partnership A nor Limited Partnership B is a publicly traded partnership. In this situation, the investor could deduct the $1,000 loss realized from one partnership against the $1,500 in income realized from the other partnership. The net result for the investor in this last case is taxable income in the amount of $500.

CHAPTER **5**

What the Securities Laws Mean to You

In Chapter 3, we looked at a very important source of rights for limited partners, the partnership agreement. The rights acquired under this agreement are contract rights, and because they are a matter of contract, they are controlled by the terms of that contract. As we saw, the rights of limited partners spelled out in typical limited partnership agreements are very circumscribed. After all, it is the general partner or sponsor of a limited partnership program that drafts the partnership agreement.

In this chapter, we are going to look at another important source of rights for limited partners: federal and state securities laws. These rights are, perhaps, much more important to an investor than those acquired under partnership law and the partnership agreement. Unlike those rights, which can be varied by an agreement controlled by the general partner, rights acquired under the securities laws cannot be altered or varied by the general partner or sponsor. The securities laws are there to protect you, the investor, the party who is dealing on what are essentially unequal terms.

Partnership Interest As a Security – Your Rights in a Nutshell

The first question you may have as an investor is why some partnership interests are subject to the securities laws in the same fashion as stocks and bonds, while other partnership interests are not. For the most part, we can safely say that all limited partnership interests are securities within the meaning of the federal securities laws. This result flows from the way in which the Supreme Court has interpreted the term "investment contract," which is one of the specific items listed as a security in the federal legislation.

According to the Supreme Court, an investment contract, and therefore a security, has the following characteristics: an investment in a common enterprise by investors seeking to profit through the skill and efforts of others. A limited partnership investment clearly meets this definition. On the other hand, a general partnership interest may not. In the case of a limited partnership interest, the limited partner or investor is seeking to profit through the efforts of the program's general partner and, in fact, is precluded for the most part from putting any of his own effort into the undertaking of the partnership. A general partner, however, exercises control over the partnership business and is likely to be looking to profit through his own efforts rather than through the efforts of others. (This does not mean that a general partnership interest could never be a security under any circumstances.)

Once a limited partnership interest is classified as a security, the partnership, its sponsors and promoters, everyone that has a part in organizing the partnership and selling interests in the partnership, as well as the limited interests themselves, become subject to the securities laws, including the Securities Act of 1933, the Securities Exchange Act of 1934, and the Investment Advisors Act of 1940. These laws and the many court decisions interpreting them are quite complex and are a very specialized area of law.

At best, we can hope only to briefly scratch the surface of these complex laws in order to acquaint you with the most important protections available to you. But before this, it may help to keep in mind that all of the federal securities laws combined are not aimed at protecting an investor from making a bad investment. Rather, the securities laws are aimed at protecting the investor by allowing him to make his own informed decisions as to the merits of an investment (1) before he makes an investment, (2) at the time of actual investment, and (3) during the period he holds his investment. The key is information, and the securities laws are aimed at disclosure:

- Before making an investment, an investor is entitled to be informed of all the factors that may affect the proposed investment and that may influence the investor's decision on whether to make the investment or not. This includes the bad as well as the good. This is a *disclosure* requirement. It is not enough for a sponsor or promoter to simply avoid providing false information, rather, he must provide *full and complete* information.

- At the time an investment is made, an investor is entitled to rely on the competence of the seller of the program. The seller should be registered to sell securities and understand the nature of the investment and the suitability of the investment for the particular investor.

- As long as the investor's investment is at risk in the hands of the general partner, the investor is entitled to be kept informed as to the progress of the undertaking and is entitled to detailed financial reports showing how the investment is being managed. The investor is entitled to be kept informed of not only those factors that are favorable to the undertaking, but to the negative factors as well.

Having summarized three major pieces of federal legislation, laws of fifty states, rules of self-regulatory professional bodies, and untold court decisions in a matter of a few short paragraphs, let's turn to some of the specifics, again with the warning that the discussion that follows is merely a "get acquainted" one, but a very important discussion nonetheless. Understanding the basic provisions of the securities laws allows you to protect your rights if a limited partnership investment goes bad through the actions of those responsible for inducing you to invest.

Securities Act of 1933

In its simplest terms, the 1933 act regulates the securities that are offered for sale to the public by requiring that the securities be registered with the SEC (Securities Exchange Commission). The purpose of this registration requirement is to force issuers of securities to provide prospective purchasers with enough accurate information so that they may make informed decisions as to whether to purchase the securities or not. Information contained in the registration statement must be reflected in the actual offering to potential investors: the "prospectus" that must be delivered to every purchaser before or at the time of the sale of every security that must be registered under the 1933 act.

Investors should clearly understand that registration of securities offered for sale to the public does *not* mean that the SEC or federal government has in any way approved of the merits of the securities or verified as accurate every item contained in the registration statement. There have been many really bad investments offered and sold to the public that were registered under the 1933 act. Remember, the act is aimed at disclosure. It may be legal under the 1933 act for a promoter to take investors' money and go to Las Vegas and gamble it away, *as long as this intention is fully and accurately disclosed* in the registration statement and prospectus.

What's more, there is no guarantee that a registered offering is completely free of fraud, although prevention of fraud in the sale of securities is the goal of the 1933 act. There have been instances when unscrupulous promoters sold outright fraudulent deals to unsuspecting investors even though the offerings were registered with the SEC. On every prospectus you will find the following warning:

THESE SECURITIES HAVE NOT BEEN APPROVED OR DISAPPROVED BY THE SECURITIES AND EXCHANGE COMMISSION NOR HAS THE COMMISSION PASSED UPON THE ACCURACY OR ADEQUACY OF THIS PROSPECTUS. ANY REPRESENTATION TO THE CONTRARY IS A CRIMINAL OFFENSE.

REGISTRATION STATEMENT AND PROSPECTUS

The registration statement that is filed with the SEC for a public offering of securities is a lengthy document that is prepared in question
and answer format. The actual registration statement is available to the
public, although most investors never see it. The bulk of the information contained in the registration statement also must be included in
the prospectus, which purchasers of registered securities *must* see. The
prospectus is presented in a narrative format. The SEC provides
specific guidelines for issuers on what must be included in a registration statement, and consequently, the prospectus.

At this point, you may wonder what value a lengthy registration
statement has if the SEC does not pass on the accuracy of the information contained in the registration. Simply put, inaccurate or omitted information provides purchasers with specific rights and may open the
issuer and others to civil and criminal sanctions by the SEC. Your rights
as an investor under the 1933 act are discussed below.

While most persons think of a prospectus as being the lengthy document that accompanies offers to sell a security, the law defines a
prospectus in much broader terms. A prospectus is any written or
broadcast material that offers a security for sale to the public. The
reason the term "prospectus" is associated with the lengthy document
is simple: every "offer to sell" must contain the information required by
the SEC to be in a prospectus. Unless all the material included in the
prospectus accompanies every offer to sell, there is a violation of the
law.

In a sense, the prospectus has something of a split personality. On
the one hand, it is a disclosure document that must disclose all material
facts relevant to the public offering of the security. On the other hand,
it is the primary sales document designed to "sell" the security to the
public. As a matter of terminology, "prospectus" is the term applied to
the sales document for a security when that security is registered under
the 1933 act with the SEC. If the security is not registered with the SEC,
the sales document may be called an "offering circular," which implies
state registration of the security, or a "private offering memorandum,"
which indicates a private placement of the securities under an exemption from the registration requirements (see the following).

Sales of securities that must be registered under the 1933 act cannot
be made legally until a registration statement is filed and has become
effective. Once a registration statement is filed, however, certain actions are permitted before the effective date. A preliminary prospec-

tus, a "red herring," may be disseminated. This document contains the material that will be in the full prospectus, but a notice, printed in red, must appear on the cover stating that a registration statement has been filed but is not yet effective. The statement also must declare that no securities can be sold and no offers to buy can be accepted until the registration statement becomes effective.

In addition to a preliminary prospectus, certain advertisements are permitted before a registration statement becomes effective. These advertisements must be very limited in what they contain and essentially are the same type of advertisements that can appear after a registration becomes effective without the advertisement being considered an offer to sell that must contain everything that must be included in the prospectus. These limited advertisements, frequently called "tombstones," may name the security and its price, how to obtain a prospectus, and who will take orders for the security.

EXEMPTIONS FROM REGISTRATION

While securities offered for sale to the public generally must be registered, there are certain classes of what otherwise might be termed public sales of securities that are exempt from the full registration requirements. Specific exemptions apply to transactions involving government securities and isolated sales of securities by individuals. Beyond these, exemptions from the registration requirements are available for offerings within a single state and offerings of limited dollar amounts of securities or sales to a limited number of investors.

The exemptions available from the registration requirements of the Securities Act of 1933 do not exempt the securities from other provisions of the securities laws, including the Securities Exchange Act of 1934. For your information, the following summarizes the exemptions available under the 1933 act and the conditions under which the exemptions apply. Limited partnership interests offered for sale under any one of these exemptions may not be offered to the public at large.

Small Offering Under Regulation A. Essentially, a "Reg A" offering is a simplified registration procedure for offerings of securities when the total offering is limited to $1.5 million. The process involves a shorter form of disclosure and takes less time and money to move through the SEC. Under Regulation A, an offering circular must be filed with the SEC and a copy of the offering circular must be given to each prospective purchaser of the security. The offering circular contains less information than is required by a prospectus in the case of an offering subject to full registration.

Private Offering Under Regulation D. A private offering or "private placement" under Regulation D is an offering of securities to not more than 35 individuals who are not "accredited investors." There is no dollar limit for a private placement, but if more than 35 investors purchase the securities, the number of investors in excess of 35 must meet the specific requirements for being "accredited investors." These requirements relate to the total dollar volume of investments made by the individuals, the net worth of the investors, and the annual net income of the investors. Suffice it to say, the requirements are aimed at limiting the offering to what might be termed knowledgeable, sophisticated investors who should be able to fend for themselves and who do not need the protections provided to the "ordinary" investor by full registration.

Investors who are not accredited investors nevertheless must understand the risks and merits of the securities, either on their own or in conjunction with a "purchaser's representative" who advises them. Nonaccredited investors must be given information in a form that essentially parallels the format of a prospectus in a full registration offering.

$5 Million Offering Under Regulation D. This exemption is another private offering exemption. The rules are similar to the private offering exemption available for unlimited dollar amounts of securities, but the up-to-35 nonaccredited investors or their representatives need not be knowledgeable and able to evaluate the risks and merits of the offering on their own.

$500,000 Offering Under Regulation D. This is yet another private offering exemption, but because of the very limited dollar amount involved, there are no specific disclosure requirements other than that there be no material omission or misstatement and that state requirements be met. Also, there is no limit on the number of investors under this exemption.

Intrastate Offering. An offering of securities entirely within a single state when the issuer, the business, and all purchasers are within the state are exempt from registration. SEC Rule 147 contains detailed guidelines that, if followed, automatically assure the availability of this exemption.

ENFORCING YOUR RIGHTS UNDER THE 1933 ACT

An investor who suffers a loss on securities acquired in a public offering may recover his loss if the registration statement contained a misstatement or omission of a material fact. Those persons who may be liable for the investor's loss include everyone who signed the registration statement, every director or partner of the issuer at the time the registration statement was filed, the underwriters, and certain professionals for those parts of the registration statement that they prepared.

A material fact, the omission or misstatement of which triggers this liability, is any information that the average prudent investor would want to know in making his decision as to whether to purchase the security or not. Liability under this provision is nearly absolute, that is, the investor does not have to prove that he relied on the registration statement. The law, in effect, presumes that if you purchase a security in a public offering that you are relying on the information contained in the registration statement. What's more, to recover, you do not have to prove that the person who omitted or misstated a material fact intended to deceive or defraud you by the omission or misstatement.

If there has been an omission or misstatement of a material fact in a registration statement, the investor is entitled to recover the difference between what he paid for the security and its value at the time of suit or what he paid for the security and the amount for which it was sold on the open market. To recover, an investor must begin his suit within one year after he discovers the misstatement or omission and within three years after the registration statement was filed.

In most cases, investors will seek to enforce their rights under the 1933 act in a class action, that is, a court suit in which all affected investors join together and seek recovery. The cost of a suit, most likely, would be too much to justify the expense for a single investor on his own.

If investors fail to bring suit within the required time period, they are not necessarily out of luck. Most likely, the same material misstatement or omission will be considered fraud under the 1934 act discussed in the next section. Proof is tougher, but more lenient time periods (statute of limitations) would apply.

In addition to the liability imposed on certain persons for misstatements or omissions of material facts in a registration statement, the 1933 act also imposes liability on persons who sell securities in violation of the registration requirements. Also, the SEC may seek an injunction or press criminal charges against anyone who, in connection with the offer for sale or sale of a security, defrauds another or uses a material omission or misstatement to obtain money or property. This latter provision does not confer additional rights on the purchaser of a security, but conduct that permits the SEC to pursue criminal charges under the 1933 act usually allows investors to sue the defendants under the anti-fraud provisions of the 1934 act.

Securities Exchange Act of 1934

If you look at the 1933 act as controlling or regulating the securities that are offered for sale to the public, then the logical extension of that are the rules of the 1934 act controlling and regulating the conduct of those involved in the purchase and sale of the securities and those who may influence a security following its sale. Some have termed the 1933 act the "paper act" (it deals with the securities themselves) and the 1934 act the "people act" (it deals with the conduct of purchasers, sellers and issuers of securities).

The Securities Exchange Act of 1934 accomplishes its goals through the registration and regulation of brokers and dealers engaged in the securities industry and the various exchanges on which securities are traded. Margin requirements issued by the SEC are formulated under the authority of the 1934 act. Also, the 1934 act is the source of the requirement for periodic reports by issuers of public securities which must disclose those facts that may affect the value of outstanding securities.

Other provisions of the 1934 act include proxy rules, short-swing profit, and insider trading rules that are not of primary concern to partners in public limited partnerships. What is of prime concern to investors in limited partnerships is the broad anti-fraud rule contained within the 1934 act.

BROAD ANTI-FRAUD PROTECTION

Section 10(b) of the Securities Exchange Act of 1934 contains a broad "anti-fraud" provision. Although it generally is termed an anti-fraud rule, its scope is much broader than traditional standards for fraud. The rule covers misstatements of material facts (traditional fraud) and omissions of material facts that are required to make what is said not misleading. The law makes it illegal, through use of the mail or any instrument of interstate commerce in connection with the purchase or sale of any security, to use any device or scheme to defraud, including any misstatement or omission of material fact or any other act that operates to defraud or deceive an individual. The statutory provision is supplemented by Rule 10b-5, issued by the SEC.

The anti-fraud rule of the 1934 act applies to any purchase or sale of a security, whether registered or not, regardless of how the purchase or sale occurs. In other words, the rule covers sales through brokers or dealers, on exchanges, or even in a face-to-face dealing between two private individuals. The misrepresentation or omission of material fact may occur in any written communication, including statements and reports filed with the SEC, private negotiations, or public or private reports to investors. False statements or omissions made by means of the telephone, even if within the same state, also can give rise to liability under Section 10(b). This list is not exhaustive, but merely illustrative of the broad sweep of the rule.

Whether a fact is material under the rule is determined by whether or not the fact would be important to the average prudent investor in deciding whether to buy, sell, or hold the security.

Unlike the rule against material misstatements or omissions in registration statements under the 1933 act, the anti-fraud rule of the 1934 act requires an investor to show that the party charged with a violation of the rule intended to deceive the investor. Also, the investor must show that he justifiably relied on the misstatement or omission in making his decision to buy or sell. Since showing reliance on an omission is difficult, the Supreme Court has created a presumption of reliance if the investor could reasonably expect disclosure of material information.

ENFORCING YOUR RIGHTS UNDER THE 1934 ACT

There is no time limit specified under the 1934 Act for bringing actions for fraud under Section 10(b). As a result, courts apply statutes of limitations found in state law, under either state securities laws (blue-sky laws) or fraud statutes.

A purchaser or seller of a security suing under Section 10(b) may seek either damages or the recision of the purchase or sale. Generally, damages are limited to what are termed "actual damages," that is, the difference between what an investor receives for securities and what he would have received had there been no improper conduct.

Just as with violations of the 1933 act, individual investors are likely to find that the cost of an individual suit under the 1934 act is prohibitive (unless a very large investment is involved). Again, the usual route for limited partners who feel that they have been the victims of securities fraud is a class action. In some cases, a derivative suit, that is, a suit brought on behalf of the partnership entity, may be brought by the partners, but this requires that the partnership be the party that suffered the damages, and it is the partnership as an entity that would recover the damages in a derivative action (although this would indirectly benefit the limited partners).

Possible Treble Damages. A statute entitled the "Racketeer Influenced and Corrupt Organizations Act" was enacted by Congress as a weapon against organized crime. The statute (RICO), in addition to various criminal sanctions, authorizes private lawsuits by aggrieved individuals to recover treble damages plus costs and attorneys' fees for violations. RICO, however, extends well beyond organized crime and can reach securities fraud, which is defined by the law as a racketeering activity. As long as there is a "pattern" of racketeering activity, which may be as little as two offenses within a ten-year period, there may be a RICO violation.

The point is that an action for securities fraud can become much more potent if it is joined with a RICO violation as well. Whether such an action (as well as any legal action) is appropriate in a given situation must be determined in conjunction with appropriate advice from legal counsel knowledgeable in the intricate provisions of the securities laws.

Investment Advisors Act

The Securities Exchange Act of 1934 required the registration of securities brokers and dealers, those actually engaged in the buying and selling of securities on behalf of clients (brokers), or from and to customers for their own account (dealers), but it left a glaring loophole. The 1934 act did not apply to those engaged in giving investment advice to others for a fee. This loophole was closed in 1940 with the passage of the Investment Advisors Act.

This act requires anyone who comes within the definition of an "investment advisor" to register with the SEC. An investment advisor is "any person who, for compensation, engages in the business of advising others, either directly or through publications or writings, as to the value of securities or as to the advisability of investing in, purchasing, or selling securities, or who, for compensation and as part of a regular business, issues or promulgates analyses or reports concerning securities." Unfortunately, the act does not require that an investment advisor show his competence, merely that he register.

Brokers and dealers who earn their fees based on the sales of securities products are exempt from the registration requirements of the Investment Advisors Act. These individuals must be registered under the 1934 act. Registration under the the 1940 act is directed at those who earn their fees solely on the basis of rendering investment advice, although a securities broker may have to register under the 1940 act if he receives separate fees for rendering advice in addition to commissions from the sale of products. There are exemptions for certain classes of individuals, such as attorneys and accountants, who are subject to other forms of regulation and governed by specific codes of conduct applying to their professions.

In addition to the registration requirements, the Investment Advisors Act also contains anti-fraud rules that may extend beyond individuals required to register under the act. These anti-fraud rules forbid conduct that acts as fraud or deceit on clients and forbid an advisor from buying or selling securities for his own account without full written disclosure to the client and the client's consent. The act also imposes an affirmative duty on an investment advisor of utmost good faith and full and fair disclosure of all material facts.

Violation of the registration requirements of the 1940 act by investment advisors, just as with a violation of the registration requirements of the 1934 act by brokers or dealers, allows the SEC to impose sanctions on the offending persons. Whether it allows an investor to recover anything, in the absence of a violation of anti-fraud rules, is open to some question. In the absence of conduct that violates the anti-fraud rules, it would seem that the most an investor could recover from a broker, dealer, or advisor required to register, but who did not register, is the fee paid to the individual. If a security was purchased from or through an unregistered individual, the investor may have the right to rescind the purchase.

State Securities Laws

In addition to the federal securities laws, the individual states have enacted their own securities regulations. Most of the state regulation closely parallels federal regulation, and many states have enacted versions of the Uniform Securities Act. Similar to the federal legislation, most state laws regulate the following areas:

1. Registration of securities to be sold within the state, including disclosure requirements.
2. Registration of individuals engaged in the securities business, including brokers, dealers, and investment advisors.
3. Anti-fraud rules that forbid the sale or purchase of securities based on false or misleading statements of omissions.

State securities laws are often referred to as "blue-sky" laws, because of the penchant of some unscrupulous promoters before the days of securities regulation for selling unsuspecting investors pieces of the great blue sky above, and very little of substance. (Whether this has changed much since regulation may be open to question.) In seeking to protect the public from such unscrupulous persons, state regulation of securities offerings often goes a bit further than federal regulation. While the federal legislation is directed at full and complete disclosure regardless of the merits of an offering, many state laws require that state securities administrators pass on the merits of an offering, allowing registration of an offering only if it is fair, just, and equitable. How much protection this affords investors, of course, is a function of the individual state securities administrations, their staffs, and budgets. In many cases, state registration can be a pro forma matter piggybacked onto federal registration.

A Word About the NASD

The National Association of Securities Dealers (NASD) is a self-regulatory body of securities brokers and dealers engaged in the over-the-counter securities market. The NASD was formed following an amendment to the Securities Exchange Act of 1934 (the Maloney Act), which authorized industry self-regulation of the over-the-counter securities market through associations registered with the SEC. The goal of the NASD is to promote fair practice by its members within the securities industry.

The NASD has promulgated Rules of Fair Practice that are designed to ensure that its members adhere to just and equitable principles in their dealings with clients. In connection with these Rules of Fair Practice, the NASD has developed detailed guidelines for various securities offerings. The NASD Rules of Fair Practice cover these essential areas:

1. Advertising. Advertisements, sales literature, and market letters must not contain promises of specific results, exaggerated claims, unwarranted forecasts of future events, suggestions that past results are indicative of future results, statements which imply NASD or SEC approval or endorsement, or statistical tables without attributing the source of the tables. Generally, advertisements should recognize that there is risk in all investments.

2. Customers. NASD members should believe that any recommendation made to a customer is suitable to the customer's financial situation. Churning, misuse of customer funds, and abuse of discretion granted by a customer, as well as other unethical practices, are also forbidden.

3. Fees. Fees and charges of NASD members must be reasonable and not discriminate among customers.

4. Bribes, Kickbacks, etc. Personnel of one NASD member firm cannot make gifts to individuals employed by another member firm in excess of a limited dollar amount. This does not bar compensation for actual services under a written contract specifying the services and compensation and acknowledged by the firm whose personnel are providing the services to the other firm.

5. Dealings with Outsiders. Generally, members of the NASD may deal with nonmembers only on the same terms as the member deals with the general public.

The NASD also has a procedure for handling complaints directed against members for violating the Rules of Fair Practice. In addition to filing a complaint that may lead to censure, fines, suspensions, or other penalties, members of the public who have a claim against an NASD member may submit that claim to arbitration under the NASD's Code of Arbitration. If a customer requests arbitration of a dispute, the NASD member must submit to the arbitration procedure.

CHAPTER 6

A Special Look
at Master Limited Partnerships

Just what is a master limited partnership (or MLP for short)? The easy answer is that an MLP is a "publicly traded limited partnership," that is, a partnership that has ownership interests, generally referred to as "units," which are traded on a recognized securities exchange or in the over-the-counter market. This easy definition has caused many investors to equate MLP units with shares of common stock. As a partnership, however, trading on the exchanges or in the OTC market may be just about the only thing MLP units and shares of common stock have in common. Investors who ignore the fundamental differences between these two investments do so at great peril to their financial well-being.

If we return to the definition of an MLP as a "publicly traded limited partnership" and examine it more critically, it tells us MLP units are traded, and therefore have some degree of liquidity, but it does not tell us more. In fact, the MLP is not a legally defined entity and the term may be a misnomer.

Rather than engage in a fruitless search for a universal definition of the term "master limited partnership," let us accept the term as a useful shorthand reference to an entire special class of limited partnership investments and turn to developing an understanding of the underlying fundamentals, a far more useful and profitable undertaking.

MLP Genesis

The beginnings of the MLP investment vehicle can be found in the explosive growth of tax shelters and tax-advantaged investments during the late 1970s and early 1980s. For various reasons, but most importantly for the tax advantage, these investments usually were structured as limited partnerships. In most cases, these investments offered little in the way of liquidity, and investors were locked in for a period of years.

Of all the many different investments packaged in limited partnership form and offered to investors as tax shelters during this period, one of the most popular was certainly oil and gas. As the price of oil shot from little more than $2 per barrel to well over $30 per barrel, oil and gas seemed like the sure ticket to riches. Even better, the tax advantages available to oil and gas investments meant that investors could make relatively sizable investments at little or no immediate out-of-pocket cash cost.

Oil exploration companies and other sponsors of oil and gas programs saw a virtually unlimited supply of capital and launched one program after the other in seemingly endless succession. Some of the programs were good, others not so good, and others were outright frauds. Nevertheless, they all had one thing in common: there was no real secondary market for the interests in the various programs acquired by the investors.

One approach tried early in the boom of syndicated oil and gas investments as a means of achieving liquidity for investors in oil and gas programs was to have the investors contribute their various limited partnership interests to a corporation. A corporation would be formed so that investors in oil and gas properties could transfer their interests to the corporation in a tax-free incorporation transaction. These corporations would provide liquidity because investors who took advantage of the swap opportunity would end up owning shares in a publicly traded corporation, rather than holding limited partnership interests.

Although the corporation could provide liquidity, it defeated the primary reasons for using the limited partnership form in the first place. Any deductions generated by the oil and gas investment that could provide a tax benefit to the investors were locked in the corporation. What's more, to the extent oil and gas income was produced, it was subject to a double tax, that is, once when earned by the corporation as corporate income, and again as individual income when distributed to the investor-shareholders as dividends.

The need for liquidity on the part of oil and gas investors, combined with the desire to retain to whatever extent possible the tax advantages of the partnership form of organization, led one sponsor, Apache Petroleum Company, to form what was one of the first, if not the first, investment packages that would later fall under the heading of "Master Limited Partnership."

In 1981, Apache offered to exchange units in Apache Partners (an MLP) for the limited partnership interests held by investors in various oil and gas programs sponsored by Apache Petroleum Company over a period of about 20 years. About 85 percent of the investors in the various Apache programs accepted the offer, and units in Apache Partners were initially valued at $20. (In the first half of 1988, Apache Partners units were trading around their record low of $3. We will have more to say on the problems of valuing units and yields associated with MLPs down the line.)

The Apache MLP thus became an early illustration of one way in which a master limited partnership may be formed: A promoter may gather together units from various partnerships under one roof. This new entity, organized as a limited partnership, continues the benefits of the limited partnership form of organization. Interests in the new partnership, however, are listed on a stock exchange and the investors achieve a degree of liquidity that they did not have prior to the formation of the master limited partnership. This type of MLP is generally referred to today as a *roll-up* master limited partnership, since smaller existing partnerships are "rolled up" into one large partnership.

It is these roll-up MLPs that probably account for the use of the word "master" in the term "master limited partnership," the idea being that a number of smaller partnerships have been combined into one "master" partnership. The publicly traded limited partnership, however, soon found many uses beyond a mere vehicle to house other partnership entities and provide investors with liquidity. But the MLP name stuck and was soon applied to any publicly traded limited partnership, even those that do not involve the combination of many subpartnerships.

Evolution and Growth of the MLP Concept

Once the idea of the publicly traded limited partnership was accepted, it wasn't long before promoters, sponsors, corporate finance experts, investment bankers, and others found many different ways to employ the concept. Although uses for MLPs other than roll-ups were emerging before the Tax Reform Act of 1986, it was this legislation, even before its passage and while it was under discussion in Congress, that spurred many to act. For the first time, individual tax rates would be below corporate tax rates, thus providing incentive for moving income off a corporate tax return and onto an individual tax return. Also, the restrictions on passive losses would create a demand for income generated by MLPs, which was thought at the time to be passive income that could be offset by passive losses from other partnership investments.

In addition to the roll-up MLPs, new MLPs were formed in a variety of ways. A corporation with substantial assets, especially real estate assets, would spin off those assets to an MLP. Shareholders who then became partners in the MLP would realize the yield from the assets in the partnership without the layer of corporate taxation that existed when the assets were held within the corporation. These MLPs, formed by a corporation transferring some of its assets to a limited partnership, are referred to as *roll-out* MLPs. In some cases, a corporation might sell units in the roll-out MLP in addition to distributing the MLP units to its shareholders.

Mature companies, those generating substantial cash income without a need to reinvest a substantial portion of that income in operations, also looked to the MLP for its potential as a tax saver. A corporation, by converting entirely to partnership form, could eliminate the corporate tax and provide its shareholders with the benefit of the lower individual tax rates on former corporate income as well. MLPs formed as a result of an existing corporation transferring all of its assets to a limited partnership are called *roll-over* MLPs.

In addition to roll-ups, roll-outs, and roll-overs, still other MLPs were formed, first to attract investor dollars, and then to acquire assets for the partnership. These MLPs formed, as it were, from scratch, are often called *roll-in* MLPs to distinguish them from the MLPs formed by existing entities for purposes other than attracting new investors.

WHY MLPs ARE FORMED

We have already alluded to some of the reasons MLPs were, and might still be, formed in the previous brief discussion highlighting how they have been formed, that is, through roll-up, roll-out, roll-over, and roll-in transactions. To better understand MLPs, a brief look at the possible motivations of the corporate general partner or sponsor in forming an MLP is in order. An investor who understands why a corporate sponsor has formed a particular MLP in the first place is in a better position to evaluate the merits of that particular MLP. In looking at the possible reasons for creating an MLP, bear in mind that they are not necessarily mutually exclusive and that many MLPs are created with several motives in mind.

Provide Liquidity. A roll-up master limited partnership provides existing limited partners with liquidity that they do not have in a conventional limited partnership. Generally speaking, limited partnerships are not liquid and limited partners have few options if they want to convert their investment into cash. Without the liquidity of a regular market, converting a limited partnership interest to cash may be accomplished only through a deeply discounted sale to the general partner or partnership or to a willing investor, if one can be found. Frequently, however, a limited partner has no ready market for his interest, even at a steeply discounted price.

Corporate Financing Tool. An MLP can be used by a corporation to obtain cash on its assets in an amount that is equal to their full value without surrendering control over the assets. In traditional financing, a lender generally lends only a percentage of the value of assets serving as collateral for the loan and may impose restrictions on the use of the assets as long as they serve as collateral. If a corporation sells assets outright to raise cash, the corporation loses control over the assets. Through an MLP, the corporation "sells" assets to the partnership for their full value, but retains control over the assets in its role as general partner. In some cases, a corporation may actually raise more cash than it would through a sale, if the market values the MLP units at a premium over the underlying assets.

Increase Shareholder Value. For a corporation that feels the market is undervaluing its stock in relation to the value of its assets, an MLP can be a way of forcing the market to recognize the full value of its currently undervalued assets. Once the assets are separated from the corporation and placed in the MLP, the value assigned to the MLP units may more closely approximate the value of underlying assets. Shareholders who obtain MLP units as part of the roll-out may sell their units and realize cash, while still retaining their ownership in the corporation and its operations.

To support a higher value for assets within an MLP as opposed to the same assets within a corporation, the assets must produce a sufficient cash flow to justify the sought-after market value.

Corporate Divestment and Capital Reallocation. A corporation may use an MLP to divest itself of assets which are no longer related to its plans or which, for the corporation, are unproductive or underproductive. The corporation can transfer its unwanted assets to an MLP and sell MLP units to the public. The cash raised can be used by the corporation to buy needed assets, reduce debt, or for any other corporate purpose.

Takeover Defense. A corporation that is the target of a takeover because of certain assets or undervalued assets may thwart the takeover by forming an MLP for the assets in question. This may increase asset values, as previously discussed, but also the corporation divests itself of the target assets and becomes the general partner with control over the assets. It may be extremely difficult for the company or persons seeking the takeover to remove the target corporation from its position as general partner of the MLP.

Supplement Shareholder Dividends. A corporation that forms an MLP and distributes the partnership units to its existing shareholders may supplement shareholder dividends with cash distributions from the partnership. Although dividends paid to shareholders following the formation of the MLP will have to be less, this can be more than made up for by the partnership distributions. Taken together, distributions to shareholders and distributions to limited partners (who are the same individuals) may exceed the amount of the earlier dividend distributions.

Reducing Administrative Costs. In the case of a roll-up MLP, a major goal of the corporate sponsor of the various partnerships that are to be combined in the roll-up is likely to be a reduction in the overhead cost involved in administering a multitude of separate partnerships. More efficient operation may lead to increased cash available for all limited partners. If good partnerships are combined with bad in an effort to save the bad, however, some limited partners may suffer.

MEANING FOR INVESTOR

As one goes down the list of possible motives for forming an MLP, it is readily apparent that corporations that have assets that are being undervalued in the market, as reflected in the market price for their stock, may have several possible motives for transferring those assets to a limited partnership and retaining control over those assets through their role as general partner. For this reason, some may be tempted to label MLPs as "asset-driven" vehicles, in that it is the value of the underlying assets that are all important in determining the value of MLP units.

In the marketplace, however, value is often a matter of the flow of income produced by assets. This will prompt others to label MLPs as "yield-driven" vehicles, that is, investments whose value are primarily determined by the cash distributions.

For the investor, however, focusing on either the underlying assets or the cash distributions may be a mistake. Certainly, the underlying assets are important, but those assets must be capable of generating sufficient cash so that the market will "correctly value" the MLP units. On the other hand, by focusing too narrowly on the cash distribution side of the equation, investors may find their "yield" actually represents a return of their own investment rather than a return *on* their investment.

In short, a good MLP investment is one in which underlying assets can support cash distributions promised by the partnership. Solid assets without cash flow may result in the same undervaluation as occurred when the assets were in corporate solution. On the other hand, cash flow without assets generating sufficient income means that the MLP is slowing but surely (or in some cases, not so slowly) liquidating itself. In this latter case, it is only a matter of time before the true state of affairs is reflected in the market value assigned to the MLP units.

At this point, however, let's not get too deeply involved with matters relating to determining return on an MLP investment. In the next chapter, we'll take a look at figuring return on limited partnership investments, including MLPs, as well as some of the "yield enhancement" techniques that may make a particular limited partnership investment appear better than it actually is.

Impact of 1987 Tax Legislation on MLPs

As discussed in Chapter 4, tax legislation enacted at the end of 1987 was directed at "publicly traded limited partnerships." MLPs, as we have seen, are just that, limited partnerships in which interests are traded on a recognized stock exchange or in the over-the-counter market. Although the tax definition of "publicly traded limited partnership" encompasses more than MLPs, it is without question that MLPs are subject to the 1987 legislation.

As a result of the tax changes, *some* MLPs are or will be treated as corporations for tax purposes, and those MLPs that are not so treated are subject to a special passive loss rule that prevents losses generated by an MLP from being used to offset income from sources other than that particular MLP. Also, income from MLPs that are not treated as corporations is considered portfolio income under the passive loss rule so that losses from nonpublicly traded limited partnerships and various tax shelters cannot be used to offset the MLP income. (See Chapter 4.)

While the 1987 tax law certainly must have an effect on MLPs, it by no means meant the end of the MLP as a viable, attractive investment in the right circumstances. The law, perhaps, is more important in what it does not do than in what it does. The law does not treat as corporations a wide range of MLPs, especially those engaged in real estate operations or natural resource operations (primarily oil and gas, although others are covered). What's more, *any* MLP in existence on December 17, 1987, cannot be treated as a corporation at least until 1998.

As for the MLPs that are not treated as corporations, the special passive loss rule should have a limited impact. Most MLPs were designed as income generators rather than as vehicles for creating tax losses, so the special loss provision is of no consequence to most MLPs. The inability of an investor to offset MLP income with passive losses from other investments may have an impact on investors heavily invested in tax shelters, but for others, this is not a factor.

In the long run, the economics of the investments that may be packaged as MLPs will outweigh whatever negative influence the tax changes have. Of course, the conversion of operating corporations to MLPs to avoid the corporate tax is no longer a viable proposition. However, the transfer of real estate and natural resource assets to MLPs as a means to enhance asset values and eliminate the potential double tax of corporate operation should continue, provided the underlying economics of the specific situation warrant it. (Real estate and oil and gas MLPs are examined in more detail in the next section.) Existing partnerships that will be treated as corporations down the line may have prices depressed by this fact. Some investors may find bargains among these issues in this environment.

CLOUDS ON THE HORIZON

There is an adage that says that if you don't like this year's tax law, wait until Congress changes it again next year. The 1987 tax legislation was aimed at changing some of the tax changes made in 1986. Looking ahead to the future, the 1987 legislation contains what might be deemed a warning of more changes to come. The warning comes in the form of a study of the tax treatment of publicly traded partnerships that the Treasury Department is ordered to undertake on behalf of Congress.

The 1987 tax legislation orders the Treasury Department, probably through the Internal Revenue Service, to conduct a study of the issue of treating publicly traded limited partnerships, *and other partnerships which significantly resemble corporations*, as corporations for federal income tax purposes. The study is to address the issues of disincorporation and opportunities for avoidance of the corporate tax.

In addition, the study must address compliance and administrative issues that relate to the tax treatment of publicly traded partnerships and *other large partnerships*. In connection with this, the study will examine imposing collection of tax at the partnership level and withholding tax at the partnership level, and will make recommendations on simplifying and improving audits and assessments of publicly traded *and other partnerships* and their partners.

Real Estate MLPs

As an investment, real estate generally has performed well over the years, offering competitive returns and a hedge against inflation unmatched by most other assets. Although most real estate limited partnerships are not publicly traded and therefore are not within our definition of an MLP, many real estate MLPs have been formed as either roll-in or roll-out partnerships. On some limited occasions, existing real estate limited partnership units have been rolled up into an MLP, but roll-ups are unusual.

For the most part, a real estate MLP must invest in or own mature properties, that is, properties that are already fully developed and producing steady rental income. As we have seen, a steady and consistent cash flow is a prerequisite if the market is to fully value the partnership units to reflect the value of the underlying real estate. This applies to MLPs of both the roll-out and the roll-in variety. As an inducement to investors, the sponsor of a roll-in MLP may set some minimum cash return to investors and agree to forego management and other fees if it is not met. The corporate sponsor of a roll-out MLP may offer a similar deal, at least for some limited period of time, in order to support the post roll-out market value of the MLP units.

A roll-up real estate MLP may end up with mature properties, but very real problems associated with rolling up existing real estate partnerships are usually too much to overcome. It is extremely difficult, if not well nigh impossible, to value different properties in different markets with different rental rates in order to set a fair exchange rate for investors who swap their existing partnership units for new MLP units. In addition, there are extremely complex tax and accounting issues that must be addressed and overcome. When a sponsor does attempt to roll up existing partnership units, it is likely to be a last ditch effort to save partnerships with troubled or distressed properties by combining them with healthy partnerships.

Still another type of real estate MLP is one formed to invest in real estate mortgages rather than in the actual real estate. Mortgage MLPs either buy existing mortgages or provide new financing to other real estate partnerships or other investors. Since the underlying assets of a mortgage MLP are mortgages and the income is derived from interest on the mortgages, the stability and safety of cash flow is usually greater than in a partnership investing in the real estate directly. Of course, this greater stability and safety should be reflected in somewhat lower returns to investors.

Mortgage MLPs, as well as other real estate MLPs, should avoid classification as corporations under the tax rules that treat many publicly traded partnerships as corporations because of the exceptions which treat interest income and any gains from the sale of assets held for the production of interest income, as well as real estate rentals and gains from real estate sales, as qualifying income. Recall that a publicly traded partnership is not treated as a corporation and that partnership tax rules apply, if 90 percent or more of the partnership's gross income is "qualifing income."

TALES OF TWO REAL ESTATE ROLL-OUTS

When a corporate sponsor rolls out real estate assets in an MLP, it may be attempting to enhance shareholder values because of the perception that the market is undervaluing its underlying assets, or it may be disposing of assets in order to raise cash for other purposes.

In what was perhaps the first roll-out real estate MLP, the corporate sponsor (Dillingham Corporation, which is now privately held) formed Ala Moana Hawaii Properties in 1981. The corporation owned two major Hawaiian shopping centers and adjacent land, 120 acres of leased land, and an additional 28 acres of land that was suitable for commercial development. At the time, the shareholders of Dillingham believed that the value of these properties was not reflected in the market value of their stock.

In order to permit the shareholders to realize full value for the real estate assets of the corporation, the corporation spun off its real estate assets by issuing units in the MLP to shareholders on a one-for-one basis, that is, each shareholder received one unit in Ala Moana Hawaii Properties for each share of Dillingham stock held. The partnership units were tradable on the New York Stock Exchange, which permitted those shareholders who wanted to realize cash on the value of the real estate to do so without having to wait until the partnership sold or disposed of the assets.

The roll-out of Ala Moana Hawaii Properties was evidently a success for the existing shareholders of Dillingham at the time the MLP was formed. Dillingham stock was trading at $12 per share before the MLP was announced. After the MLP was announced, share prices rose to $35, and after the MLP units were issued, the units traded at about $21.50 and the stock at about $13.50 (reflecting the combined value of $35 realized because of the roll-out of the real estate assets in the MLP).

Clearly, the underlying value of the corporation's real estate was not reflected in the price of its stock and the MLP permitted investors in the corporation to ultimately realize this underlying value. While the Ala Moana MLP was directed at allowing existing shareholders to realize the value of the underlying real estate held by the corporate sponsor, Burger King Investors MLP presents another and far different use of a real estate MLP by a corporate sponsor.

Pillsbury Company, Burger King's parent, formed Burger King Investors in 1985 and sold 98 percent of the interests in the partnership to the public. Pillsbury formed the MLP by "selling" 128 Burger King restaurants (both owned and leased) to the partnership. Units were sold to the public for $20 per unit, and Pillsbury raised over $86 million after commissions and expenses of the offering. The gain realized by Pillsbury from the "sale" of the restaurants permitted it to report a 30 percent jump in pretax profits, rather than a 30 percent drop for the quarter in which the MLP was formed.

While Burger King, through its parent Pillsbury, raised a good deal of capital from what ostensibly was a sale of some of its properties, Burger King did not actually give up control over those properties. In effect, Pillsbury and Burger King employed the MLP as a very sophisticated financing tool. Pillsbury, with its 2 percent interest in the partnership, served as general partner. Burger King was permitted to continue to lease the restaurants from the partnership as long as it wanted, but the partnership could not, on its own behalf, terminate a Burger King lease. In addition, if percentage rents raised the income to the partnership significantly, a provision in the partnership agreement automatically increased the share going to the general partner, Pillsbury.

The point of the two stories of these real estate MLPs is not the specifics involved in each of the roll-outs, but rather simply to illustrate that MLPs can be, and are, formed for a variety of different reasons. One real estate MLP is not necessarily the same as another. Investors must bear in mind that sponsors have different motives for being willing to cut investors in on their own version of a "good investment." Examine the motives and reasons why a particular MLP is being formed *before investing*. Knowing this, you will be better able to evaluate both the merits of the offering and any special risks entailed.

Oil and Gas MLPs

The search for oil and gas is an expensive proposition. The cost of locating drill sites and drilling exploratory wells is high, especially now that the "easy oil" has been found. Some industry estimates project that only one out of every ten exploratory wells will result in the find of a new field. On top of this, perhaps only one out of forty or fifty exploratory wells will actually result in a field that is a significant commercial success. These figures clearly explain why outside investors are sought by professional oil and gas operators. If a commercially successful well was a "sure thing," or maybe even a fifty-fifty proposition, there would be more than enough money from insiders to finance all oil and gas exploration.

But oil and gas is a risky business, outside investors are sought, and MLPs are just one vehicle for raising money from investors to finance the search for oil and gas. Of course, when we are talking about raising new money from investors for an oil and gas MLP, we are talking about a roll-in MLP. In our brief discussion of the various underlying investments for most limited partnerships in Chapter 2, the point was made that investors should know the prospects on which the program's sponsor intends to drill. With an oil and gas MLP, this may be difficult. Most roll-in MLPs that will engage in oil and gas exploration are formed as blind pools, in much the same fashion as roll-in real estate MLPs. Investors in roll-in oil and gas MLPs must have a high degree of confidence in the ability of the corporate general partner.

In addition to possible roll-in MLPs, MLPs of the roll-up and roll-out variety are also common in the oil and gas industry. In either case, the MLP will be set up with existing producing wells. The Apache program, a roll-up MLP, was examined previously in the discussion of the beginnings of the MLP investment vehicle. It may be considered typical of a roll-up oil and gas master limited partnership. In any roll-up, good partnership units are blended with mediocre partnership units, and this is no less true for oil and gas than any other underlying investment.

In a roll-out oil and gas MLP, a corporation transfers producing oil and gas properties to a limited partnership. The partnership units may be distributed to existing shareholders as a way of allowing shareholders to realize full value on what may be undervalued assets and to avoid the double tax on oil and gas income that occurs when that income is realized by a corporation and then must be distributed as dividends to individual shareholders. Mesa Partners was formed initially by Mesa Petroleum Corporation as a means of distributing the royalties on its oil and gas properties to its shareholders without subjecting the royalties to corporate tax.

Roll-out MLPs in the oil and gas area also may be employed by the corporate sponsor to sell off producing properties in order to realize the cash for further exploration or in order to diversify out of the oil and gas business. As soon becomes apparent, roll-out MLPs, whether in oil and gas, real estate, or some other area, may be formed by their corporate sponsors for a variety of reasons. Again, one of the keys to evaluating the merits and risks of a roll-out oil and gas MLP is getting a handle on the motives of the corporate sponsor for rolling out its producing properties.

Regardless of how an oil and gas MLP was formed, all existing oil and gas MLPs remain viable in the public markets because they contain producing properties that are producing a cash flow. The cash flow is dependent on the production from the wells, and the level of cash flow is dependent on the price of oil and gas in the commodities markets. Investors should never lose sight of the fact that an investment in an oil and gas MLP is an investment in a commodity. A fall in the price of oil and gas translates automatically into lower payouts and a decline in the value of partnership units. By the same token, a rise in oil and gas prices means a virtually automatic increase in the value of partnership units. A time of depressed petroleum prices may be a time to bargain hunt among oil and gas MLPs.

Another very important point to keep in mind regarding the cash flow from oil and gas MLPs is that cash flow is provided at the expense of future income. Most oil and gas MLPs produce more oil and gas than they find to replace their reserves. Cash going to partners cannot be used to explore for and find new reserves. Cash flow going to the partners ultimately means that the partnership is, in effect, liquidating itself. An MLP that provides a lower level of payout may be capable of making payouts over a longer period of time. You should keep this in mind when comparing and evaluating various oil and gas MLPs.

Why Invest in an MLP

In deciding whether an interest in an MLP belongs in your portfolio, you may want to consider the possible advantages this investment vehicle has over traditional limited partnerships and other investments. Consider the following.

Economics. The possibility of economic profit should be foremost in your mind. The underlying investments for MLP programs, particularly oil and gas and real estate, may offer what you consider to be the opportunity to realize a greater return than other investments at the time you are considering the investment. Other limited partnerships may offer the same, but of course, economic conditions change, and the MLP offers you the opportunity to adjust your portfolio.

Liquidity. This is the obvious advantage that MLPs offer over other limited partnership programs. You can buy, sell, hold, and margin your MLP units in much the same fashion as your investments in common stock. Of course, liquidity varies from one MLP to another and the depth of the market for the particular units involved. The reasons why an MLP was formed in the first place often affects the actual liquidity of an MLP.

For instance, a roll-up MLP may result in a flurry of trading following its formation since the limited partners previously had been locked into their earlier partnership investment. Trading may dry up once this initial activity subsides. Roll-out MLPs, when units are distributed to shareholders, may experience a similar trading pattern as shareholders seek to realize on the corporate assets spun off to the MLP. Other roll-outs and roll-ins may have a more stable trading volume after the initial sale of units to the public. An initial valuation for a roll-out that is too generous, however, may mean trading at a price below the initial offering price.

Diversification of Underlying Assets. The MLP, because of its size, may offer a greater diversification in the underlying investments of the partnership. This, however, is not necessarily true, and each MLP should be evaluated to determine the degree of diversity involved. For instance, a real estate MLP may have different types of properties in many different regions of the country. On the other hand, it may have similar properties widely dispersed, such as Burger King Investors, or diversified properties in a single area or region, such as Ala Moana, or even similar properties in a single region of the country.

Reinvestment or Current Income. Generally, most MLPs have been oriented to provide current income or cash flow at the expense of reinvestment. Nevertheless, not all MLPs are the same in this regard. Investors can choose among MLP investments that offer higher current income with reduced reinvestment, or MLPs that reinvest a portion of their income in order to provide investors with a longer-term investment. You should consider the investment objectives of any particular MLP you are considering and be sure that those objectives fit your desire for a long- or short-term investment, depending on your own investment goals.

Tax Benefits. MLPs that are not treated as corporations offer most of the tax benefits of traditional limited partnership investments. There is but a single tax at the investor level to reduce the return from the underlying assets of the partnership. In addition, as a partner, you are entitled to a return of your cost (tax basis) before cash distributions to you become taxable in addition to the flow-through of partnership income as a result of the conduit nature of the partnership. Of course, you receive the benefit of any tax rules that defer the tax on income realized by the partnership, including depreciation and depletion.

Special Basis Adjustment. Because of its complexity, many MLPs may not offer a special, elective, basis adjustment that is available under the tax law. This election is referred to in tax jargon as the "Section 754 Election."

Essentially, if the partnership has this election in effect and you pay more for your interest in the partnership than the book value of that interest in the partnership, the partnership is permitted to step up the book value of partnership assets that relate to your interest in the partnership. This can increase the tax deferral on partnership income to the extent the partnership's assets are subject to depreciation, depletion, or other deductions determined on the cost or other adjusted tax basis of those assets.

In considering an MLP investment, you must remember that each MLP program is a unique investment. The factors previously noted apply generally to all MLPs, but they do so in unequal fashion. It is impossible to say whether an "MLP investment" is right for you without considering the specific nature of the particular MLP involved and the economic conditions existing at the time. Even though MLPs are publicly traded, the investment is still essentially an investment in the underlying assets owned by or to be acquired by the partnership. What may be a liquid investment at the time you make the investment in real estate, oil and gas, or anything else for that matter, may prove highly illiquid if you want to sell at a time of depressed prices or economic slump affecting the underlying assets.

CHAPTER 7

Figuring Your Return:
How to Avoid
the Blue Smoke and Mirrors

Regardless of the investment, we must proceed from one simple fact: No investor is a font of unlimited cash with which to make investments. You must choose between investments that are competing for your investment dollars. This is true whether you have $5, $50, $5,000, or even $5 million to invest. Of course, an investor with $5 million may have more choices than an investor with $5,000, but choices, nevertheless, must be made. All other things being equal, you will choose to invest in a limited partnership only if it provides you with the opportunity to earn a greater return in line with your investment objectives than other investments that are available to you. This brings us to the question of how to figure your return from a limited partnership and compare that return to that from available alternatives. There are many measures of return to lead or mislead.

If you wanted to sum up the way to measure return from a limited partnership, you could say that it is simply a matter of looking at the estimated cash flow from the investment and comparing that cash flow to the cost of the investment. You would decide to invest only if the risks and returns are suitable for your personal and financial situation.

Of course, this is much easier said than done, but it is more or less objective. In "going through the numbers," however, don't lose sight of some of the more subjective elements of a limited partnership investment. For instance, don't overlook the experience, competency, and integrity of the general partner. An inept general partner can destroy an otherwise valuable limited partnership, and a dishonest promoter can cheat hundreds or thousands of investors. But we will have more to say on this topic in the remaining chapters. For now, let's concentrate on the more objective elements in judging a limited partnership investment.

Some Basics

Figuring your potential return from limited partnerships and comparing that return to investment alternatives begins with two very fundamental principles. The first principle is that more is better than less. To put it in numbers, it is better to have $200 than $100, so that an investment that returns twice as much as an alternative investment is the one to choose. But if we stop here without considering the second, and equally important, principle, we easily will be mislead.

The second principle is that now is better than later. Only if this second principle is considered along with the first can we accurately discern the "more from the less." For example, the "more is better than less" principle, standing alone, tells us that $110 is better than $100. But if we factor in the second principle, what appears at first glance to be more (the $110) may, in fact, be less.

If I know that I can put $100 in the bank and earn 6 percent interest, then $100 "now" is "more" than $110 two years "later." This conclusion flows from what is termed the "time value of money," that is, the ability of money to earn more money over time. By putting $100 in the bank today at 6 percent interest, I know that in two years time I will have $112.36, assuming that the interest is compounded on an annual basis.

Of course, this type of analysis is looking to the future. In making investment decisions, we must be concerned with today. I have $100 right now, today. A limited partnership investment offers me $112.36 two years from today if I invest that $100. Should I make the investment? By using the reverse of compounding, called discounting, we know that $112.36 two years from now is the same as $100 today, provided I can earn 6 percent on that $100. [In financial terms, $100 is the present value (PV) of $112.36 in two years discounted at 6 percent.] If alternatives don't provide me with the opportunity to earn at least 6 percent, then I know that the limited partnership offers me the potential for a greater return on my $100. I am, of course, left with the decision of whether the higher return is sufficient to justify taking any greater risks that may be associated with the limited partnership, but that is another question.

We now have the necessary basic tools to evaluate and compare returns from limited partnership investments. Let's develop our two fundamental principles a little further and see how various measures of return can mislead us into poor investment decisions, as well as lead us into the right decisions.

SIMPLE ACCOUNTING RETURN

One of the most widely used measures of return is the simple accounting return. This is the total profit from an investment divided by the cost of the investment, with the result divided by the number of years of investment. The result under this analysis will be the same regardless of whether after-tax or pretax figures are used, provided the tax rates and assumptions remain the same as to cost and profit. If this is not the case, then after-tax figures should be used to reflect the effects of taxes on the investment. For example, suppose an investor could invest $5,000 and receive $10,000 back in two years. Further assume that the cost of the investment is deductible at the investor's combined state and local tax rate of 40 percent and that the entire $10,000 return also is taxed at 40 percent. The annual accounting return, using pretax figures, would be 50 percent, calculated as follows:

Cash returned	$10,000
Cost of investment	(5,000)
Profit	$ 5,000

$5,000 profit/$5,000 cost = 1.00/2 years = 50%

Using after-tax figures, the result is the same:

Cash returned	$6,000
Cost of investment	(3,000)
Profit	$3,000

$$\$3,000 \text{ profit}/\$3,000 \text{ cost} = 1.00/2 \text{ years} = 50\%$$

If the cost of the investment were not deductible and the profit were taxed at our assumed 40 percent tax rate, the accounting return would be 30 percent calculated as follows:

After-tax cash returned	$8,000
After-tax cost	(5,000)
After-tax profit	$3,000

$$\$3,000 \text{ profit}/\$5,000 \text{ cost} = 0.60/2 \text{ years} = 30\%$$

An investor who uses the simple accounting return to measure return is taking into account our first basic principle, that more is better than less, but is ignoring our second principle. Simple accounting return ignores the time value of money, our second principle that now is better than later. This can be illustrated very effectively by comparing the investment of $5,000 fully deductible dollars returning $10,000 fully taxable dollars at the end of two years with a fully deductible $5,000 that would return $5,000 after one year and $5,000 after two years. In both cases, the annual accounting return is the same, 50 percent:

$$\$5,000 \text{ total profit}/\$5,000 \text{ cost} = 1.00/2 \text{ years} = 50\%$$

Given a choice between an investment that (1) returns $10,000 at the end of two years or one that (2) returns $5,000 at the end of one year and $5,000 at the end of two years, however, you would choose the second, despite the identical accounting returns. By choosing the second investment, you know that you can have $5,000 working for you, earning interest, for one whole year longer than would be the case with the first choice. Being able to earn 5 percent simple interest after taxes on this $5,000 for one year means that the second investment puts $250 more in your pocket than does the first investment.

Looking only at annual accounting return does not reflect this critical difference. Since limited partnerships provide cash flow in different amounts at different times in the life of the investment, accounting return cannot be used to figure *accurately* your return or to compare limited partnerships with alternative investments.

PAYBACK PERIOD

Payback period is another common method of comparing limited partnerships to alternative investments. The payback period is the time required for the after-tax income from the investment to equal the after-tax cost of the investment. The idea behind this measure is that the sooner you get your investment back, the better the investment.

This measure of return reflects our second basic principle that now is better than later. Unfortunately, it completely ignores our first principle, that more is better than less. While considering to some degree the time value of money, payback period can be grossly misleading because it does not take into account any return after the payback period as well as the consequences of selling or other termination of the investment. Compare the following investments, each with a cost of $5,000. One has a payback period of three years, the other a payback period of four years. The investment with the longer payback period is clearly the better alternative.

	Returns	
Year	*Investment #1*	*Investment #2*
1	$2,000	$2,000
2	2,000	1,000
3	1,000	1,000
4	0	1,000
5	0	5,000
Payback	3 years	4 years

While Investment #1 returns your cash outlay in only three years compared to Investment #2's four years, your obvious choice is Investment #2 as the better alternative. The time value of money in this case cannot possibly make up for the extra return realized from Investment #2 after the payback period.

The examples of accounting return and payback period just presented are, of course, quite simple, and any limited partnership will present a more complex picture of cash flows than that presented. The possible distortion in the wealth building potential of a limited partnership investment when the measure of return used ignores either the quantity of dollars returned or the time value of those dollars, however, remains the same. Let's move on to ways of figuring return that do take into consideration both of our fundamental principles.

Understanding Internal Rate of Return (IRR)

A method frequently used to measure return from a limited partnership investment is what is known as the internal rate of return, or IRR. IRR is defined as the discount rate that, when applied to an investment, results in the sum of the present values (PV) of the costs and the benefits of the investment equaling zero. For example, an investment that costs $3,790 and pays back $1,000 per year at the end of each of the following five years has an IRR of 10 percent, illustrated as follows:

Year	Cost or Benefit	PV at 10%
Investment	($3,790)	($3,790)
1	1,000	909
2	1,000	826
3	1,000	751
4	1,000	683
5	1,000	621
		$ 0

This measure of return does take into consideration both of our basic principles, that more is better than less and that now is better than later. While IRR can be an effective tool in judging limited partnerships, you must understand its limitations and drawbacks. If you do not, IRR merely becomes another measure of return that can mislead rather than lead.

While IRR does take into account the time value of money, it must be calculated with the aid of a computer or calculator programmed to do IRR calculations. Figuring IRR without the aid of these devices is a tedious and time-consuming trial-and-error proposition. After the cost and expected benefits of the investment are determined, they are discounted to present values at some arbitrary interest rate. If the sum of the present value of the costs at this assumed interest rate is less than the sum of the present values of the benefits at this rate, a higher rate of interest must be used. If the sum of the present values of the benefits is less than the sum of the present values of the costs at this rate, a lower rate of interest must be used. The IRR of the investment is eventually arrived at by zeroing in on the correct rate in this fashion.

Difficulty in calculating IRR without computer assistance may not be much of a drawback today, considering the general availability of such devices. Nevertheless, there are other considerations. In some cases, there may be more than one IRR for the same investment. This can be the case whenever there are costs (negative cash flows) in years other than the year of investment. While many public limited partnerships are designed to avoid this occurrence, it is not all that unusual. Tax rules combined with borrowing by the partnership can produce a tax liability in a future year that is, in effect, a recapture of taxes deferred in an earlier year.

Whenever multiple IRRs are indicated, it is possible to develop a single IRR through the use of a sinking fund approach that eliminates the future negative cash flow by offsetting that negative amount with the positive cash flow of earlier periods. With the future costs offset in this fashion, only a stream of benefits is left (up to the point that the sinking fund must kick in to offset the future costs) on which IRR may be calculated. Since your author is not a mathematician, he has no desire to even attempt to get into more detail on this subject. Rather, you are referred to other works if such mathematical detail is desired. What we are concerned with is understanding the concept of IRR and what it means when applied to a limited partnership.

WHY IRR IS NOT EQUIVALENT TO CURRENT YIELD

Perhaps the biggest mistake made by investors looking at IRR figures for a limited partnership investment is equating IRR with yields on bonds or other securities, or even interest rates on bank deposits. IRR is *not* a current or bank yield. Rather, IRR is an annual yield on un-recovered investment, that is, it reflects both the rate of return *of* capital and the rate of return *on* capital. As a result, an IRR figure is higher than, and not comparable to, a bond's yield to maturity or the rate of interest on a time deposit. How this can be misleading is illustrated by the following example comparing two investments.

EXAMPLE. Assume there are two investments available to you at an initial cost of $10,000 each. Investment #1 has the following flow of costs and benefits:

Year	Cost or Benefit
Initial Investment	($10,000)
1	1,000
2	1,500
3	2,000
4	9,296

Investment #2 has the following flow of costs and benefits:

Year	Cost or Benefit
Initial Investment	($10,000)
1	6,000
2	4,800
3	1,400
4	406

After completing the tedious IRR calculations for these two investments, you would find that Investment #1 has an IRR of 10 percent and that Investment #2 has an IRR of 15 percent. Despite the higher IRR for Investment #2, 50 percent higher in fact, your better investment choice may be Investment #1 with its lower IRR.

The apparent contradiction in the preceding example stems from the fact that IRR assumes that all benefits from an investment are being reinvested at the same rate. In other words, the 15 percent IRR for Investment #2 assumes that the $6,000 recovered in year 1 is reinvested at that 15 percent, an unlikely proposition. Your capital recovery on Investment #2 is so fast that there is very little left in the investment that the 15 percent rate operates on. In the case of bond yields or rates on time deposits, your earnings are, in effect, being reinvested at the same rate, that is, there is no capital recovery until the end of the investment period.

The same assumption in IRR calculations, that benefits are reinvested at the same rate, may also cause confusion in another way. An IRR of one investment that is twice as high as the IRR of another does not mean that an investor will realize twice the economic benefit by choosing the former. Again, the higher IRR is assuming reinvestment at the higher rate. For instance, an investment with an IRR of 20 percent is assuming that your opportunities for reinvesting the flow of funds from the investment will be 20 percent, while an investment with an IRR of 10 percent is assuming that your opportunities for reinvesting the flow of funds from the investment will be only 10 percent. In other words, IRR is saying that your reinvestment possibilities are conditioned on the initial investment that you choose, a very unlikely and unrealistic proposition.

Let's go back to the previous example and compare the results under two different assumptions as to your ability to reinvest the benefits from your initial investment decision. In one case, we will assume you can reinvest the benefits flowing from your initial decision at a rate of 8 percent and in the other case, we will assume a reinvestment rate of 5 percent.

EXAMPLE. Assume you can reinvest the benefits of Investment #1 or #2 from the previous example at 8 percent. At the end of the four-year period, you would have $14,465 as a result of choosing Investment #1, but $15,075 as a result of choosing Investment #2:

Investment #1:
$1,000	for 3 years at 8%	= $ 1,260
1,500	for 2 years at 8%	= 1,749
2,000	for 1 year at 8%	= 2,160
Final amount		= 9,296
Total		=$14,465

Investment #2:
$6,000	for 3 years at 8%	= $ 7,560
4,800	for 2 years at 8%	= 5,597
1,400	for 1 year at 8%	= 1,512
Final amount		= 406
Total		=$15,075

Under this assumption as to your ability to reinvest the benefits from your initial investment choice, the higher IRR did indicate the better choice.

Now assume that instead of reinvestment at 8 percent, you are able to reinvest the benefits from your initial investment choice at only 5 percent. Under this assumption at the end of the four year period, you would have $14,208 as a result of choosing Investment #1, but only $14,114 as a result of choosing Investment #2:

```
Investment #1:
    $1,000        for 3 years at 5%      = $ 1,158
     1,500        for 2 years at 5%      =   1,654
     2,000        for 1 year at 5%       =   2,100
     Final amount                        =   9,296
  Total                                  = $14,208

Investment #2:
    $6,000        for 3 years at 5%      = $ 6,946
     4,800        for 2 years at 5%      =   5,292
     1,400        for 1 year at 5%       =   1,470
     Final amount                        =     406
  Total                                  = $14,114
```

Under this assumption as to your ability to reinvest the benefits from your initial investment choice, the higher IRR failed to indicate the better choice.

USEFULNESS OF IRR

The Internal Rate of Return is a useful tool when comparing two very similar investments as long as the limitations and drawbacks to this method are remembered. First, you must remember that IRR does not equate to yield to maturity or interest rates often used to measure return on other types of investments. Second, all assumptions used in the calculations of IRR for different investments must be the same. And never overlook the assumption implicit in all IRR calculations: that the benefits flowing from the investment may be reinvested at the same rate.

Since it is this last point that often causes the most problems with using IRR to figure return on limited partnership investments, adjusting IRR to reflect a realistic return on reinvested benefits may provide a better picture of true return. Most investors have some idea of a "safe" rate of return that they can achieve. This rate may be a rate on insured bank deposits or various Treasury securities. By substituting this rate as the reinvestment rate, calculating the future value of each annual benefit flowing from an investment when reinvested at this rate, and then calculating IRR on the basis of the cost of the initial investment and the future value of the reinvested benefits, a more realistic assessment of a particular limited partnership investment may emerge.

Regardless of the method chosen to evaluate a possible limited partnership investment, it cannot provide the ultimate answer as to whether to invest or not. The accuracy of the results must depend on the accuracy of the projections as to the prospective costs and benefits of the investment. You must still evaluate the economic, financial, and tax risks of a proposed limited partnership investment in light of your particular investment objectives. With this caveat in mind, let's look at still another method of evaluating limited partnership investments, use of net present value.

Using Net Present Value

In order to use net present value as the measure of worth of a limited partnership investment, all costs and benefits are converted to their present value (PV) at some assumed interest rate. This can be done with the aid of a financial calculator or any calculator with the aid of a table of present value factors.

The first problem is what interest rate to use as the discount factor in converting costs and benefits to present value. As previously noted, everyone has some idea of what he can receive on relatively safe investments, such as insured deposits or Treasury instruments. This is one rate that can be used. Also, since limited partnerships are alternatives to other investments, you can use the rate of return on your current investment portfolio. If one of these rates is used, you can compare a proposed limited partnership investment with safe alternatives or your current return on your investments. Following this procedure, you can tell if a limited partnership makes economic sense if the investment performs as indicated by projections. If you can't beat your current return with a limited partnership even if it performs as expected, then you can eliminate it from consideration as an investment alternative.

EXAMPLE. Let's assume that two investors have the opportunity to invest in a real estate limited partnership. The sponsor expects the partnership to operate the properties it is to acquire for eight years, at which point the properties will be sold and the proceeds distributed to the partners. The after-tax costs and benefits for the two investors are presented in the following cash flow schedule. The difference in costs and benefits for the two investors may be accounted for by a difference in federal and state tax rates and other tax rules applicable to each investor. Otherwise, the investment by each is identical. (Year 1 is assumed to be the current year, the time when the investment is made.)

Year	Investor #1	Investor #2
1	($5,000)	($6,200)
2	0	0
3	2,019	1,620
4	1,879	1,507
5	1,761	1,419
6	1,617	1,303
7	1,595	1,285
8	1,569	1,265
9	(577)	23
Total	$4,763	$2,222

As is apparent from the cash flows, both Investor #1 and Investor #2 will make money on this limited partnership investment, if the cash flow projections are accurate. But the reason to make the investment is to achieve a greater return than could be obtained through alternative investments. Suppose both investors can realize 8 percent on other "safe" investments (or are netting 8 percent on their current investments). Does it make sense for either investor to purchase an interest in this limited partnership?

The way to determine this is to reduce the cash flow (the series of costs and benefits) to its net present value using the investors' alternative rate as the discount rate. If the result is positive, the limited partnership offers a greater return than the investor can achieve with alternative investments. If the result is negative, the investor would be better off with alternative investments. Reducing the cash costs or benefits the investors expect to present values at 8 percent produces the following net present value for each investor:

Year	Investor #1	Investor #2
1	($5,000)	($6,200)
2	0	0
3	1,730	1,389
4	1,492	1,197
5	1,295	1,043
6	1,100	888
7	1,005	810
8	915	738
9	(312)	12
Net Present Value	$2,225	($ 133)

As you can see, Investor #1 would be better off by making the investment in place of alternative investments, if the projections prove to be accurate. This investor can now evaluate the reasonableness of the projections and the extra risks associated with this limited partnership (see "Considering Risks" on page 110). Investor #2, however, would not be better off making this investment in lieu of alternative investments, even if the limited partnership performs as expected. Investor #2, therefore, can eliminate this limited partnership investment from his investment considerations.

COMPARING INVESTMENTS USING NET PRESENT VALUE

In addition to providing a means of assessing a single limited partnership interest, net present value also can be used as a selection tool in choosing between two or more possible limited partnership investments which are competing for your investment dollar. Once you have established that several limited partnerships offer the potential for a better return than your alternative rate, you can select the investment that has the highest net present value at the alternative rate as providing you the best return.

EXAMPLE. Assume that you want to choose between two limited partnership investments. The projected after-tax cash flow (costs and benefits) from these two investments are as follows:

Year	Investment #1	Investment #2
1	($ 7,500)	($ 7,500)
2	1,500	2,000
3	500	3,000
4	13,500	10,500
Total	$ 8,000	$ 8,000

The net cash flow from both of these investments is the same, $8,000. Converting the costs and benefits to present value at an assumed alternative rate of 8%, however, shows that one investment will provide a slightly better return than the other, if both perform according to the projections:

Year	Investment #1	Investment #2
1	($7,500)	($ 7,500)
2	1,389	1,852
3	428	2,572
4	10,719	8,337
Net Present Value	$ 5,036	$ 5,261

As long as the projections for these two investments prove to be accurate, Investment #2 would provide a greater return than Investment #1. All other things being equal, you would choose Investment #2 over Investment #1.

While reducing costs and benefits to net present value provides a method for assessing the potential value of a proposed limited partnership investment and a means of comparing competing investments, the point must be stressed that it cannot provide the ultimate answer as to whether to invest or not, any more than the IRR method can provide such an ultimate answer. You must always evaluate the economic, financial, and tax risks associated with any proposed limited partnership investment in light of your own objectives.

CONSIDERING RISKS

In using net present value as a means of judging return on a limited partnership investment, the first problem encountered was selecting an appropriate discount rate to use in the calculations. In the previous examples, the rate chosen was an alternative "safe" rate or the rate being earned on current investments. In using one of these rates, there is an implicit assumption that the risk involved in the limited partnership is the same as that on the alternative investments. In fact, this is unlikely to be the case. Most limited partnership investments entail more risk than an assumed "safe" return, such as that which can be obtained on insured deposits, Treasury instruments, or even tax-exempt bonds.

If you use an alternative safe rate to discount the projected costs and benefits of a proposed limited partnership investment and the result is positive, you have learned that you might do better with the limited partnership than the alternative investment, but you haven't learned whether your potential return is sufficient to overcome any extra risks entailed with the limited partnership. There are different ways of taking additional risk into account, but when using the net present value method to assess a proposed limited partnership investment, perhaps the easiest is simply to increase the discount rate used to reduce costs and benefits to their present values.

It is very difficult, if not impossible, to actually quantify risk in some objective fashion. Nevertheless, in studying a proposed limited partnership investment, reading the sales literature and the prospectus, looking at the partnership agreement, learning about the sponsor or general partner and its past successes or failures, you should develop some intuitive feel for the extra risks involved. This evaluation, of course, will be subjective. However, you would not be comfortable investing unless you believed that the potential existed for earning a sufficient return to overcome any extra risk involved, *as you perceive that risk.*

EXAMPLE. Let's assume that you are considering a limited partnership investment and that your "safe" rate is the rate you could earn on tax-free municipal bonds (this is an easy rate to use because it is automatically an after-tax rate of return). At the time, this alternative rate is 5 percent. Your initial investment in the limited partnership would be $5,000 and the investment is projected to produce the following after-tax costs and benefits, with year 1 being the current year of investment:

Year	Cost or Benefit
1	($5,000)
2	500
3	1,000
4	1,000
5	5,000
Total	$2,500

This limited partnership investment will be profitable if it performs as projected but can it beat your alternative rate? You convert the costs and benefits to net present value at your alternative rate of 5 percent:

Year	PV of Cost or Benefit
1	($5,000)
2	476
3	907
4	864
5	4,114
Net Present Value	$1,361

You now know that if this limited partnership performs as projected, you can beat your alternative rate. But what of the risk that the projected returns won't be achieved? After studying everything you can about this investment, you decide that there is twice as much risk involved than would be the case with a 5 percent municipal bond, or put in another fashion, that you would not be comfortable making this limited partnership investment unless the potential existed for doing twice as well as you could with your alternative investment. So, you discount the costs and benefits at twice the alternative rate, or 10 percent:

Year	PV of Costs and Benefits
1	($5,000)
2	455
3	826
4	751
5	3,415
Net Present Value	$ 447

Since the net present value of the costs and benefits is positive, you know that you can achieve your desired return as adjusted for the risk that the investment will not perform as projected. In other words, the potential rewards of this investment compensate for the risks as you perceive them. If you were uncomfortable with the risks even with the potential for a return twice as great as your alternative investment, you might choose a higher discount rate, say three times your alternative rate, or 15 percent:

Year	PV of Costs and Benefits
1	($5,000)
2	435
3	756
4	657
5	2,859
Net Present Value	($ 293)

Since the net present value in this case is a negative number, you know that this investment could not achieve your desired return as adjusted to compensate for the perceived risks. If you would be comfortable with this investment only if there was the potential for doing three times as well as with a municipal bond, you would reject this investment.

Of course, any results achieved in the process just outlined are far from exact. What the process is doing, however, is giving you a feel for the particular limited partnership and how it might fit within your investment plans. It is a relatively simple process and not very time consuming in itself. Perhaps its biggest advantage lies in getting you to really think about any proposed limited partnership investment and to look at whatever information is available to you, including income projections and what lies behind those figures. Before moving on to other topics, let's explore some of the ways limited partnership sponsors may make yields look better than they actually are through what are sometimes called "yield enhancement" devices.

Artificial Yield Enhancement

In order to attract investors, limited partnership sponsors sometimes resort to devices that make yields on limited partnerships appear better than they actually are. Turning to the prestidigitator's art, a limited partnership sponsor may resort to blue smoke and mirrors to make potential investors see what is not and not see what is. Sometimes a limited partnership investment promises high current cash flow *plus* appreciation, but in reality is providing an inflated current cash flow at the risk of the total return on the partnership investment.

What are some of these "yield enhancement" devices that may encourage you to invest unless you carefully analyze exactly what is being offered? While we certainly cannot cover every possibility that may be thought up by overeager limited partnership sponsors, we can look at some general patterns that have been used to create the illusion of above-market yields. Essentially, the devices fall within three general categories:

1. Cash flow to investors that exceeds the actual cash flow to the partnership.

2. Cash flow to investors that actually represents a depletion of their capital.

3. Cash flow to investors that is temporary and that will disappear down the line.

Let's look at a few of the yield enhancement devices that fall in these general categories.

DISTRIBUTIONS IN EXCESS OF "REAL" CASH FLOW

One way limited partnership sponsors can make yields on limited partnerships appear greater than they actually are is by paying out more to limited partners than is justified by the actual cash flow to the partnership. This does not mean that the partnership pays out $10 for every $9 coming in on a current basis. Rather, what is done is what might be termed borrowing from tomorrow in order to make cash distributions today. One way a limited partnership might borrow from tomorrow is to defer debt payments until partnership assets are sold or partnership property is refinanced at some point in the future. Regardless of the mechanics chosen to accomplish this, the hope must be that partnership property will appreciate sufficiently and at a fast enough rate to cover the deferred debt and interest.

Zero-coupon bonds or other debt instruments can be used to make current cash flow to limited partners higher than what is justified by actual conditions. Zero-coupon debt is essentially debt on which no principal or interest payments are made until the debt matures. With no debt amortization, there is more current cash available for distribution. Of course, the interest on the debt is compounding so that the amount due when the debt matures is significantly higher than the original amount borrowed. For instance, a 10 percent interest rate will result in a doubling of the debt in something like seven-and-one-half years, about the average projected lifespan of many real estate limited partnerships. In other words, if a partnership borrows $1,000 at 10 percent using a zero-coupon obligation, the obligation grows to $2,000 in only seven-and-one-half years. Cash from rentals or other operations can be distributed to limited partners instead of meeting current interest and principal amortization payments, but the debt must be satisfied some day.

Instead of zero-coupon debt obligations, other borrowing arrangements may be employed to accomplish the same results. For instance, an "accrued-interest mortgage" is about the same as zero-coupon debt. When accrued-interest financing is used, the borrower may agree to a higher overall rate of interest, but is obligated to actually pay some lower amount for an initial period with the rest of the interest compounding until maturity. Again, the idea is to have cash that would (or should) otherwise go to make interest and principal amortization payments available for distribution to limited partners.

Regardless of the name used to describe this type of financing, the danger to limited partners is clear. If there is insufficient appreciation in partnership assets, either real or as a result of general price inflation, to cover the debt plus accrued interest, there will be less available for the limited partners when the partnership winds up and is liquidated. While the higher cash flow to investors might have made the limited partnership appear to provide a better return, the overall return may be lower than that available on alternative investments when the final distributions are considered.

In addition to deferring debt, other charges or fees can be delayed or deferred in order to artificially inflate the current distributions to limited partners. For instance, the general partner or sponsor may avoid or delay collecting fees due it under the partnership agreement until the limited partnership is liquidated or refinanced somewhere down the road. Of course, at that time the general partner will collect the fees or charges *plus* interest on the accrued amounts. Again, the effect is the same, more cash today for distribution but less available later. The higher current distributions may make the partnership return appear better than will ultimately prove to be the case.

EXAMPLE. You are offered the opportunity to invest in a real estate limited partnership that will own and operate rental property. The properties will be acquired for cash and are essentially fully rented so that your share of rents for a $5,000 investment will be $500 after all operating expenses but before the general partners 10 percent "management fee." The management fee is disclosed in the prospectus and partnership agreement, but the partnership agreement also gives the general partner the right to defer collecting its fees and allows 10 percent interest on all deferred amounts. By deferring the fees, the partnership is able to distribute $500 to you annually. This cash distribution, when compared to your $5,000 investment, provides an apparent 10 percent return.

Now suppose that your alternative rate was something less than 10 percent. You might be tempted to consider this investment because of its apparent 10 percent return. A present value analysis, however, will reveal that your actual return from this limited partnership will be less than the apparent 10%. Let's assume that the partnership will operate for five years and that there will be no appreciation in the value of the partnership's assets. The actual cash flow from this partnership would be as follows:

Year	Benefit or Cost
Initial Investment	($5,000)
1	500
2	500
3	500
4	500
5	5,195
Total	$2,195

The final year's cash flow represents your original investment (with no appreciation) plus the rent from the final year reduced by the deferred $50 management fee from each year plus accrued interest on the fee. Reducing the costs and benefits of this investment to present value at 10 percent reveals that the apparent 10 percent return as a result of the $500 annual distributions is, in fact, a false measure of return.

Year	PV of Benefit or Cost
Initial Investment	($5,000)
1	455
2	413
3	376
4	342
5	3,226
Net Present Value	($ 188)

Another way of looking at this is that the present value of your $5,000 investment at 10 percent is only $4,808, that is, if you assume a 10 percent return, you are receiving only $4,808 in exchange for your $5,000 investment, which is exactly the present value at 10 percent of what you would have received had the general partner taken out his $50 fee each year and distributed only $450 to you in each year plus $5,000 at the end of five years.

Regardless of what expense or obligation is deferred, the effect is the same: To boost current cash distributions, which makes your return appear greater, at the cost of future benefits, which causes your return over the entire life of the partnership to be less. When considering any limited partnership that seems to offer above average yields for the type of underlying investment, look for deferred debt repayment or deferred charges or fees of any type that may account for what appears to be a greater than average yield but, in fact, is not.

DEPLETING CAPITAL

Closely related to techniques that borrow from tomorrow in order to make cash distributions today are another range of yield enhancement devices that return the investors' own capital in a way that makes it seem that the return on the partnership investment is higher than it actually is.

In discussing why Mesa Petroleum went to a limited partnership, T. Boone Pickens said that it was no longer desirable at that time to protect Mesa Petroleum's reserves and that "if in fact you're not going to protect it and are going to deplete it, you'd better put it into the best possible structure ..." In other words, what Mr. Pickens was saying was that the limited partnership structure provided a good vehicle to slowly liquidate Mesa Petroleum. Mesa was not going to invest its cash flow to develop new oil and gas reserves, but rather was going to distribute that cash flow. Part of that cash flow represented the capital initially invested in developing the oil and gas reserves and once fully depleted, would leave the former shareholders, now limited partners, with nothing of value in the partnership.

You can relate this idea to any limited partnership that invests in natural resources. If you invest $5,000 in an oil program, that $5,000 represents the cost of the oil in the ground. As the oil is extracted and sold, cash is produced which is distributed to you. Part of that cash is your original investment (the cost of acquiring the oil in the ground), so if some of the partnership's cash flow is not reinvested, part of each dollar you receive represents a return *of* your investment and part represents a return *on* your investment. For example, if you receive $500 annually on your $5,000, it appears as if you are receiving a 10 percent return. But if part of each $500 represents a return of part of your $5,000 initial investment, your real return is less than 10 percent, perhaps much less, depending on how fast the partnership is depleting its capital in the form of oil reserves.

Natural resources are not the only investments that lend themselves to yield enhancement through capital depletion. Almost any investment made by a limited partnership can be made to appear more attractive in terms of current distributions by simply not reinvesting sufficient cash flow to maintain the value of the original investment. Real estate, for instance, may deteriorate through neglect or insufficient maintenance caused by excessive cash distributions. In effect, the foregone maintenance in such a case represents a return *of* the investors' original investments, not a higher real return *on* their investments.

Still another yield enhancement technique that involves capital depletion or disguising a return of investment as a return on investment is the use of excessive cash reserves, set up on formation of a limited partnership, to provide a fund from which distributions can be made to limited partners. All general partners will hold back a certain amount of cash, and not invest every cent that comes in from investors, in order to meet unexpected contingencies. This is merely prudent and good business practice. However, if these reserves are more than what are called for by the investment, they may be used to boost cash payouts to the limited partners and thus make the return on the limited partners' investment appear greater than what it actually is.

Sometimes this payback of a limited partner's own capital through these techniques is promoted as a benefit, as a "tax-deferred yield." But remember our discussion on the tax treatment of limited partnerships. All distributions are tax free to the extent of basis or cost. If a limited partnership is distributing more than it is earning, that excess is tax free because it is a return of the investor's own money, not taxable income. While certain tax rules, most notably depreciation and percentage depletion, do allow a true tax-deferred yield because the tax expense is not a true cash expense, you should carefully examine any "tax-deferred yield" to ascertain its source. Be on guard for investments returning your own money disguised as a current return on your investment.

DISAPPEARING CASH FLOW

The final group of artificial yield enhancement devices that may be employed in limited partnerships include those in which cash flow is created through some act of the general partner or sponsor and which will disappear over time or at some future date. The high initial cash flow makes the investment appear attractive, but careful scrutiny reveals that it is unlikely that high current distributions can be maintained for any length of time.

One technique often employed is the sale-leaseback. Under such an arrangement, the sponsor sells property to the limited partnership and agrees to lease the property back at a guaranteed rent for a certain period of time. This initial rent may be artificially high simply to induce investors to invest. At the end of the leaseback period, when the property must be rented to third parties, it may be impossible to obtain the same high rents. The decline in rents, of course, means that all or some of the cash flow to investors must dry up.

There doesn't even have to be an actual sale-leaseback. The rental may be to subsidiaries or other entities related to the general partner and sponsor of the limited partnership. Pillsbury entered into such an arrangement in connection with its setting up of the Burger King Investors partnership, which was discussed in Chapter 6. Something as simple as a guarantee of a certain level of rents for investors that expires at the end of a set period of time can accomplish the same result.

Mortgage partnerships also lend themselves to the "disappearing cash flow" technique. Some mortgage partnerships lend money to other limited partnerships or buy existing mortgages, but other mortgage partnerships lend to other troubled partnerships of the same sponsor. Interest on loans to other partnerships of the same sponsor may be above market, but can the partnerships support the payments required? In effect, if you invest in the latter type of mortgage partnership, you are assuming risks that no commercial lender is willing to assume. Your high return may simply disappear in a rash of bankruptcies and foreclosures.

Conclusion

When you invest in a limited partnership, you are looking for cash flow, but not cash flow that has no more substance than blue smoke. Cash flow from a limited partnership should be predictable and steady. You must look behind the cash flow to ascertain its true source. Is it a return *on* your investment (good) or a return *of* your investment (not so good)? Constructing a cash flow analysis for the *entire life of the investment*, and converting that cash flow to present value at your alternative rate, or alternative rate adjusted for added risk, is a good way of getting a handle on your potential return and the nature of that return.

Remember, a high current cash return as a percentage of your initial investment may simply be a debt created against tomorrow, a return of your own capital, or a temporary phenomenon as a result of some act of the general partner. The inquiry forced on you by a net present value analysis may show whether your apparent high return is real, or an illusion created with blue smoke and mirrors; whether a limited partnership offers the opportunity for you to achieve a real economic profit, or an investment in which only sponsors and general partners stand to gain.

CHAPTER **8**

Comparing the Limited Partnership to Other Familiar Investments

You can own income-producing assets, such as real estate, natural resource deposits, leased equipment, and even an operating business, either directly or indirectly through an equity interest in some intermediary entity. If you own the property directly, you generally have full control over the property, you can buy and sell at will (subject to finding a willing buyer, of course), you reap the income produced by the property (and pay the taxes), you suffer the full effect of any losses, and are fully responsible for any debts or liabilities that arise in connection with the property. For most investors, direct ownership is simply not a practical alternative for the ownership of most income-producing assets. In the first place, the amount of money necessary to acquire direct ownership of many assets would shut the door on a great number of opportunities for all but the wealthiest of individuals. In the second place, there is the matter of time. Unless you are willing to devote your full time to the management of the assets, for instance, as the proprietor of a going business, it is unlikely that you can reap the full potential from the assets that you do own.

The twin constraints of limited resources and limited time force us to turn to various indirect forms of ownership. The limited partnership, the subject of this book, is one form of indirect ownership, but there are others that may be familiar to you to one degree or another. In all cases, indirect ownership alters our ability to manage and control assets, to buy and sell the assets, and to obtain the income produced by the assets (and to pay the taxes). In addition, indirect ownership alters our potential liabilities as holders of the assets. The differences, of course, vary from one form of indirect ownership to another, and some of the differences are favorable while others are unfavorable.

In this chapter, we take a brief look at the various forms of indirect ownership of income-producing assets. Following this is a more detailed look at those specific equity investments that may be considered more likely alternatives to limited partnerships: common stock and real estate investment trusts (REITs). Each of these is compared and contrasted with the limited partnership as to (1) management and control, (2) liquidity and marketability, (3) income and taxation, and (4) liability of holders. Finally, a brief word is presented on the "real estate mortgage investment conduit" (REMIC), a creature created by Congress in the tax law, that may be structured as a partnership, corporation, or trust, but that has only one set of tax rules applicable to it regardless of its legal form of organization.

Indirect Ownership of Income-Producing Assets

Investors may acquire ownership of income-producing assets indirectly by acquiring an ownership interest in a corporation, a partnership, or a trust. Generally, the corporation stands at one end of the spectrum, that most distant from direct ownership. The partnership stands at the other, closer to direct ownership. The trust is somewhere in the middle. Of course, any such classification is a matter of generalities, since variations in ownership interests within each entity cause the boundaries to blur and overlap. This is now more true than ever as hybrid forms of ownership proliferate and securities are developed that split ownership into ever more narrowly defined interests.

Before looking at these forms of indirect ownership, a bit of explanation is in order. In this brief overview, it certainly would be possible to classify the various entities based on any one of the four factors set out above, that is, management and control, liquidity and marketability, income and taxation, or liability of holders. The federal tax code, however, does provide us with a universal system (at least as far as the United States is concerned) of classification. For this reason, and the fact that more readers will at least find the classifications somewhat familiar, I have chosen income and taxation as the prime classification category. With this in mind, let's look at indirect ownership through separate taxable entities, conduits, and partial conduits.

SEPARATE ENTITIES – THE CORPORATION

By acquiring ownership of corporate stock, an investor acquires indirect ownership of income-producing assets owned by the corporation. Corporations may hold investment property or engage in the active conduct of a trade or business. For income and tax purposes, corporations are treated as separate entities apart from their shareholders. Income earned by the corporation is taxed to the corporation. For the most part, shareholders have no right to compel the corporation to distribute that income to them, unless they control a majority of the shares. The management of the corporation, entrusted to the board of directors, is free to decide the best use for corporate income, that is, reinvestment in the corporation or distribution to shareholders. If corporate income is distributed to the shareholders, it is treated as separate income that has not yet been taxed. In other words, when the shareholders receive a distribution of corporate income, they pay taxes on that income, even though the corporation, as an entity, has already paid taxes on that very same income.

This "separateness" of a corporation carries over into the other areas, most importantly, in the area of liability of holders. The corporation and its shareholders are separate as to potential liability. A corporation's shareholders (with the possible exception in certain instances of controlling shareholders in a closely held corporation) cannot be held liable for the debts, obligations, and any other liability that falls upon the corporate entity. By the same token, the assets of the corporation cannot fall to claims against shareholders. The shareholder's interest in the corporation may be subject to claims against the shareholder, but those with such claims cannot reach the assets within the corporation.

Carrying the idea of "separateness" further, management of the corporation, but not ultimate control, is removed from the shareholders. Shareholders elect the board of directors to manage the affairs of the corporation. The shareholders do not exercise day-to-day control over the management of the corporation, but a majority can influence management through their ability to elect the board of directors. The degree of this ultimate control is a matter dependent on how concentrated or diffuse share ownership is.

For the most part, marketability and liquidity again point to the separateness of the corporate entity from those who own it. Shares of stock (absent special restrictions) are freely transferable. All shareholders may sell their stock so that there is a 100 percent change in ownership over the corporation, yet the corporation remains undisturbed. Its business continues, its contracts and legal obligations are unaffected. Of course, this is the theory. While corporate stock is theoretically liquid and freely marketable, the degree is dependent on there being willing buyers for any stock interest offered for sale by the current shareholder. This is not a problem for corporations listed on the exchanges or over the counter, barring some major financial or economic crisis.

All this is the general nature of indirect ownership through a corporate entity. It is not true for all stock ownership in all corporations. Preferred stock and other classes of voting and nonvoting stock, shareholder agreements and restrictions, indemnity and hold-harmless agreements, can alter many of the rights and obligations of shareholders in general. The most likely form of corporate ownership to compete with an interest in a limited partnership for an investor's consideration is the full equity ownership represented by a common stock interest. Ownership of common stock is compared and contrasted with ownership of a limited partnership interest in some detail in a later section.

CONDUITS

The general partnership is the form of indirect ownership that comes closest to direct ownership as to all four of the factors that we are considering. As we have seen, general partners manage and control the partnership and are exposed to potential liability for any debts or liabilities incurred by the partnership. Partners have the right to their shares of partnership income and pay taxes on their shares. The partnership as an entity does not pay taxes on income earned by the partnership. The liquidity and marketability of a partnership interest are usually quite restricted because the consent of other partners is required to admit a new partner. The close identity of the partnership with its partners carries over in the tax rule that considers a partnership as terminated for tax purposes whenever there is a more than 50 percent change in ownership.

The general partnership is not really an alternative to the limited partnership as a form of indirect ownership for investors. As we have seen, the limited partnership alters the management and control and potential liability of limited partners while preserving the conduit nature of the partnership as to income and taxation.

In addition to the partnership, there is another form of indirect ownership that operates as a conduit, the S Corporation. This entity is a creature of the tax law and for all purposes *except taxation* is treated as a regular corporation. Income earned by an S Corporation is taxed to shareholders whether distributed or not in a way that is similar to the taxation of partners in a partnership. Except in certain instances, the S Corporation does not itself pay taxes on the income earned by the corporation.

The conduit nature of the S Corporation combined with the other features of a corporation would make it an ideal form of indirect ownership in many cases. Unfortunately, the tax law places severe limits on the corporations that can qualify as S Corporations. Only corporations with 35 or fewer shareholders may qualify. This restriction alone eliminates use of the S Corporation as a vehicle for offering indirect ownership of income-producing assets to large numbers of the investing public and, accordingly, as an alternative to the limited partnership. It has been used, however, in a limited number of private offerings. The 35-shareholder limit for an S Corporation coincides with the limit placed on offerings to nonaccredited investors in a private offering exempt from full SEC registration under Regulation D.

PARTIAL CONDUITS

A trust is a form of indirect ownership that is a partial conduit. A trust is an arrangement under which trustees take title to property and become responsible for the protection and conservation of that property on behalf of the indirect owners, the beneficiaries. The trust is a partial conduit because the trust, although a taxable entity, does not pay tax on income distributed to beneficiaries. Essentially, income retained by the trust is taxed to the trust and income distributed is taxed to the beneficiaries. With a regular corporation, all income is taxed to the corporation, whether distributed or not, and with a partnership, all income is taxed to the partners, whether distributed or not.

As a form of indirect ownership for investors, however, the trust is simply not a practical alternative to the limited partnership. Under the tax law, if a trust is used for carrying on a profit-making business that ordinarily would be carried on through a business organization such as a corporation or a partnership, the trust is not treated as a trust for tax purposes, but rather is considered an association taxable as a corporation. There is an exception that allows a trust that holds income-producing assets to be treated as a trust, but only if there is no power under the trust agreement to vary the investment.

Real Estate Investment Trust (REIT). The real estate investment trust is a form of indirect ownership for real estate assets that does offer an alternative to the limited partnership. In general, an entity may qualify as a REIT if it is a trust or a corporation with at least 100 different freely transferable interests and if it would be taxed as an ordinary domestic corporation if it did not meet the REIT requirements. These requirements relate to the composition of the entity's assets, which must be substantially real estate assets, and the entity's income, which must be realized in a substantial part from certain real estate and real estate related sources.

The ability of a REIT to engage in regular business activities is limited by the requirement that income from the sale or disposition of stock or securities held less than one year, or real property held less than four years, must be less than 30 percent of the REIT's income. Also, a 100 percent tax is imposed on income from the sale of property held for sale to customers in the ordinary course of trade or business, other than foreclosure property.

An entity that meets the requirements and elects to be treated as a REIT generally is treated as a partial conduit. A REIT is generally subject to the regular corporate tax, but receives a deduction for dividends

A REIT cannot directly manage the properties that it owns, but it must employ independent contractors. Operations of the REIT must be overseen by a board of trustees, of which a majority must be "outside" trustees under the NASAA guidelines. These restrictions may help protect the interests of investors (who have ultimate control to the same extent as shareholders of a corporation), but they do greatly limit the operating flexibility of a REIT.

Limited Partnership Interest. In contrast to the REIT, the limited partnership has a wide degree of latitude in which to operate, and the general partner or sponsor can effectively retain control over the assets of the partnership. Some investors may view this as a detriment. However, the flexibility retained by the general partner to make investment decisions with few restrictions allows the limited partnership to be an investment vehicle that is potentially more responsive to changing economic and market conditions. In the hands of a competent general partner, this flexibility can be an advantage to investors.

LIQUIDITY AND MARKETABILITY

REIT. Interests in REITs may be freely traded without impact on the REIT. Owners are free to buy and sell REIT interests without restrictions. REITs, however, have gone through several periods in which their liquidity was more apparent than real. Troubled real estate investments by some REITs in the past have made interests virtually untradable (since nobody wanted to buy) at one time or another.

Limited Partnership Interest. Interests in real estate limited partnerships, for the most part, are relatively illiquid, and investors must continue to hold their interests for the five- to ten-year projected life of most real estate partnerships. The exception is real estate master limited partnerships, which are designed to be publicly traded. At any time, however, the market for a real estate master limited partnership interest may be so shallow that a sale can be achieved only at a substantial loss of capital.

INCOME AND TAXATION

REIT. A REIT may serve as a conduit for income from real estate, but it must distribute 95 percent of its income to shareholders. A REIT cannot reinvest earnings and retain its status as a REIT. This limits the capital growth potential of a REIT. Also, as a partial conduit, a REIT serves as a conduit for income, but losses and deductions realized by a REIT do not flow through to provide a tax benefit to investors.

Income from a REIT is considered portfolio income under the restrictions on the use of passive losses, so passive losses cannot be used to offset income from a REIT. Tax-exempt institutions may realize income from a REIT without the imposition of the unrelated business income tax.

Limited Partnership Interest. The treatment of income and taxation of a limited partnership was developed in the preceding section. The limited partnership is a complete conduit, so, unlike a REIT, losses, deductions, and credits, in addition to income, pass through to the limited partners. Also, the general partner retains a great deal of discretion as to whether to distribute partnership income or retain it within the partnership. This does allow the limited partnership to retain and reinvest income when the general partner deems it appropriate for the preservation of partnership capital and investments.

LIABILITIES OF HOLDERS

REIT. The owner of an interest in a REIT generally has no personal liability for the obligations and liabilities of the real estate investment trust.

Limited Partnership Interest. The owner of a limited partnership interest, in a fashion similar to the owner of an interest in a REIT, generally has no personal liability for the obligations and liabilities of the partnership. The owners of a general partnership interest, however, generally are personally liable for the obligations and liabilities of the partnership.

A Word About REMIC

In the Tax Reform Act of 1986, Congress provided special tax rules for what it dubbed "real estate mortgage investment conduits" or "REMICs." In general, a REMIC is a fixed pool of mortgages with multiple classes of interests held by investors. *Any entity*, including a corporation, partnership, or trust, that meets specified requirements may elect to be treated as a REMIC. Also, a segregated pool of assets may qualify as a REMIC as if it were a legal entity, provided the necessary requirements are met. In short, the REMIC is a replacement entity for limited partnerships, REITS, and mutual funds that in the past have invested in real estate mortgages.

INVESTORS' INTERESTS

As long as the requirements now specified in the Internal Revenue Code for qualification as a REMIC are met, the REMIC is not treated as a separate taxable entity. Rather, the income of the REMIC is allocated to, and taken into account by, the holders of interests in the REMIC. These interests are divided into "regular interests," which can be further divided into more than one class, and a single class of "residual interests."

The terms of a regular interest in a REMIC must be fixed and unconditionally entitle the holder to receive a specified principal or similar amount and base interest or similar payments, if any, at or before maturity on a fixed rate. (A variable rate may be used under regulations specified by the Internal Revenue Service.) These regular interests may be issued in the form of debt, stock, partnership interests, interests in a trust, or any form of legal organization that is permitted by state law.

A residual interest is any interest in the REMIC other than a regular interest, and which is so designated by the REMIC. There can be only one class of residual interests, and all distributions, if any, made to holders of residual interests must be made on a pro rata basis.

TAX TREATMENT OF REMICs AND HOLDERS

A REMIC is not a taxable entity for federal income tax purposes. The income of a REMIC generally is taken into account by holders of regular and residual interests as briefly described in the following paragraphs. This conduit feature of the REMIC applies regardless of whether the REMIC otherwise would be treated as a corporation, partnership, trust, or any other legal entity. In enacting the REMIC provisions into the tax law, Congress wanted them to be the exclusive set of rules for the treatment of all transactions relating to the REMIC and holders of REMIC interests, if the requirements for REMIC status are met by the entity. For instance, a REMIC that is organized as a partnership and that would be treated as a partnership under the tax law if there were no special REMIC provisions, is not treated as a partnership if the REMIC requirements are met. In such a case, the partnership tax rules do not apply to any transaction involving the REMIC or to any holders of interests in the REMIC.

The holder of a regular interest generally is taxed as if his regular interest were a debt instrument to which the rules of taxation applicable to debt instruments apply, except that the holder is required to report income attributable to the regular interest on the accrual method of accounting regardless of his regular method of accounting. In the case of a regular interest that is not an actual debt instrument, the amount of the fixed unconditional payment is treated as the stated principal amount of the instrument, and the periodic payments, if any, that are based on the amount of the fixed unconditional payment are treated as stated interest payments. In other words, consistent with the conduit nature of the REMIC, the holders of regular interests generally take into account that portion of the REMIC's income that would be taken into account by an accrual method holder of a debt instrument with terms equivalent to the terms of the regular interest.

The holder of a residual interest in a REMIC takes into account as ordinary income his daily portion of the taxable income or net loss of the REMIC for each day during his taxable year in which he held the interest. The taxable income or net loss of the REMIC for determining this pass-through is figured in the same way an individual using accrual accounting would figure his calendar-year taxable income, but with certain modifications. The most important modification is that the REMIC deducts amounts that would be deductible as interest if the regular interests were treated as indebtedness of the REMIC. This provision, in effect, prevents the holders of residual interests from being taxed on income allocable to the regular interests.

Actual distributions from the REMIC are not included in the income of a residual holder to the extent distributions do not exceed the holder's adjusted basis for his interest. Distributions in excess of basis are treated as income from the sale of the residual interest. The amount of any net loss of the REMIC that may be taken into account by the holder of a residual interest is limited to the holder's adjusted basis. Any loss disallowed as a deduction because of this provision may be carried over and used in the future, but only to offset future income generated by the same REMIC.

These rules on the treatment of the income and loss of a REMIC allocable to residual interests closely parallel those applicable to partnerships, as discussed in Chapter 4. The method of determining the adjusted basis of a residual interest is also similar to the method of determining the basis of a partnership interest. A holder's initial basis (cost) is increased by the amount of taxable income of the REMIC that is taken into account by the holder. The basis is decreased, but not below zero, by the amount of any distributions received from the REMIC and by the amount of any net loss of the REMIC that is taken into account by the holder.

Essentially, what Congress said in passing the REMIC provisions is that no matter how an investor makes an indirect investment in a pool of mortgages, the tax treatment will be the same. Regardless of whether an investor acquires an interest in a pool of mortgages through a real estate limited partnership, a REIT, or a mutual fund, if the investor's interest has the characteristics of debt, it will be treated as debt for tax purposes. On the other hand, if the investor's interest has the characteristics of a sharing of profits and losses, that is, an investment in which the investor is assuming the position closely akin to that of a limited partner, the interest in the REMIC will be treated in the same fashion as a partnership interest for tax purposes.

CHAPTER 9

Planning a Partnership Investment Program

By now you have some understanding of the limited partnership as an investment vehicle. This means that you are ready to begin the hard work. The limited partnership offers you an investment alternative, another opportunity to put your capital to work. But you must be willing to take the time and expend the effort that is necessary to evaluate potential limited partnership investments. If you are unwilling to do this, your experience with limited partnerships, regardless of the underlying assets of the partnerships you choose, is bound to be disappointing at best, catastrophic at worst.

After all is said and done, limited partnerships are just another form of investment; it requires work to select an investment that offers a reasonable opportunity for profit. Like common stock, a more familiar investment, limited partnerships offer good, bad, and mediocre opportunities. You cannot guard against an investment turning sour because of economic conditions or other factors beyond your control or the control of the managers of your investment, but you can protect yourself against your own hasty or ill-considered decisions and from apparently incompetent partnership management.

In all likelihood, you would not make an investment in common stock before you sized up the outlook for the industry in which the company is a player and the possibilities that the company would perform better than others in the same industry. Why should you do any less when it comes to limited partnerships? In fact, there is even more reason to scrutinize carefully a possible limited partnership investment than an investment in common stock. In a rising stock market, there is the possibility of gain, even if the particular company in which you have invested is performing below comparable companies. In most cases, this market effect is not available to help an otherwise poor performing limited partnership.

There is another important point that emerges from the idea that limited partnerships are just another form of investment which can be expected to produce good and bad results. The way a stock market investor handles the possibility that some stocks will prove to be losers despite his best efforts to evaluate his stock selections is through diversification. Diversification is also a good strategy for limited partnership investments. If you can continue a carefully planned investment program over a period of years, you are less likely to suffer a major loss than if you invested in a single limited partnership.

Sizing Yourself Up

Before considering specific limited partnership investment opportunities, you might want to consider whether limited partnerships in general are suitable in light of your own financial and personal situation and temperament. This self-analysis not only can steer you away from limited partnerships if they are not for you, but if you conclude they are worth considering, also can help you pinpoint the types of limited partnerships that offer you the best opportunities.

AMOUNT AND TYPE OF INCOME

The first step in deciding whether limited partnerships may be right for you is a careful appraisal of your income, and not just the dollar amounts involved. You must consider all aspects of your income picture, including predictability, sources, and tax treatment, in addition to the actual amount of your yearly income. Obviously, if you are spending all your income just to maintain your lifestyle, you cannot consider limited partnership investment opportunities. Your first goal if you find yourself in this position is to reorder your spending priorities and to begin a regular savings program that can provide a base for meeting unexpected needs and a future investment program.

The amount of disposable cash you have can also influence the type of investment you should consider. Some investments require larger cash outlays than others, and it would be foolish to stretch your investment budget simply to invest in a limited partnership.

Another factor you must consider is the predictability of your income. Before investing in a limited partnership, you should have a fairly clear picture of what your income will be over the next several years. Generally, once you invest in a limited partnership, other than a publicly traded partnership, you can become locked in for several years. If you are unsure of your future income, you don't want to commit yourself to a several-year investment. Should future conditions require you to pull out of a limited partnership investment prematurely, you may find the cost of getting out to be so high that it is not worth the effort, providing you can get out at all.

The predictability of your future income is also important if you want to pursue a diversified partnership investment program. You must be reasonably sure of your future income so that, once you begin your diversified investment program, you can continue that program.

You also must examine the sources and types of your income and how it is affected by income tax laws. Remember, a limited partnership is a conduit and the income, losses, deductions, tax credits, and, in fact, everything that can affect an individual's tax calculations, flow through from the partnership directly to the partner's tax return. Accordingly, partnership tax items affect the partners' individual tax items, and the partners' individual tax items affect their shares of partnership tax items. Since no two investors are identical as to their tax positions, a limited partnership that can achieve certain results for one investor will not necessarily achieve those same results for another investor. Your own particular "tax profile" can alter the results achieved for you by a particular limited partnership investment.

You must examine all the factors that affect the calculation of your tax liability. Of course, the marginal tax rate to which you are subject is important, and not just for the current year, but for all years up to the time a partnership program is projected to end. Projecting your future tax rates, just as projecting your future stream of income, may require a bit of crystal-ball gazing, but it is necessary to get a handle on how you can expect a partnership investment to perform for you. And don't forget state and local income taxes in addition to federal taxes. In some areas, these taxes are considerable and can affect the comparative after-tax results of different investments that are subject to different tax treatment.

In addition to tax rates, the sources and types of your income are important. For instance, tax preferences can subject you to the minimum tax. If you have tax preference income from other sources, you may want to avoid investments that will produce additional tax preference income. Passive income can be offset with deductions from passive activities, but other types of income cannot. Your deductions are also important. Different deductible items have limits or floors. You must consider how partnership deductible items passed through to you from the partnership will affect the deductions you have from other sources. In some cases, you may not get the full tax benefit from certain deductions, while in other cases, additional deductions may provide a tax benefit because they push the total over a floor amount.

LIQUIDITY

In addition to the amount and type of your income, you also must assess your liquidity before beginning a limited partnership investment program. You should not divert liquid assets, such as cash or marketable securities, to limited partnership investments if you may have need of the funds in an emergency. Even a limited partnership that would otherwise make economic sense may not be the right investment for you if you may need your liquid assets for emergency or other purposes.

As we have noted, limited partnerships, with the general exception of master limited partnerships, are illiquid investments. Many limited partnerships restrict the right of partners to freely transfer their partnership interests in order to preserve their partnership tax status. Again, with the exception of master limited partnerships, there generally is no real secondary market for limited partnership interests. So, even if there are no restrictions on the transfer of a particular limited partnership interest, you may be hard put to find a willing buyer for your interest in a limited partnership.

Adding to the potential liquidity problems of a limited partnership investment are the possible adverse tax consequences that may arise in certain cases from a premature disposal of a limited partnership investment. The tax problems can be especially acute if the partnership leveraged its underlying assets. In some cases, even if a sale can be arranged, the sale may not produce a single cash dollar for you.

RISK

Limited partnerships, as a general rule, are more risky than many other investments. If this were not so, there would be no need for limited partnerships generally to offer the opportunity for higher returns. If you make an investment in a limited partnership, you must be prepared for the possible loss of your investment. This possibility exists no matter how carefully you examine and evaluate the underlying investment to be made by a partnership and the management and operation of the partnership itself. Evaluations of limited partnerships must be made on the basis of assumptions and projections that are subject to a wide margin of error. If you cannot afford to lose money invested in a particular limited partnership, you should simply not invest. This serves to highlight once again the importance of diversification to guard against the complete loss of your capital.

Another aspect to consider in regard to risk, one which really goes beyond the self-analysis with which we are presently concerned, is the effect changing economic conditions can have on limited partnership investments. Your outlook can greatly influence your investment decisions. For instance, if you foresee declining oil and gas prices, you certainly would not want to invest in an oil and gas limited partnership. On the other hand, if you think oil and gas prices will rise in the future, you are more likely to invest in an oil and gas partnership, even though current prices might make such an investment appear less attractive than others.

Economic conditions also effect alternatives to limited partnership investments. There may be times when economic conditions may make some alternative investments more attractive to you. Market conditions cannot be ignored, and the same considerations that affect all your investment decisions must affect your decisions with regard to limited partnerships.

TEMPERAMENT

A final point to consider in your analysis of the suitability of limited partnership investments as alternatives for you is your temperament. Conventional wisdom tells us that some individuals are simply not cut out to invest in the stock market. For these individuals, the daily ups and downs of the market are too much for them, and they cannot watch the continuous price fluctuations without panicking at the first sign of a downturn. Or perhaps they cannot accept their losses when they make a poor stock pick. Maybe they hold on to their favorites long after the time to sell has passed them buy. These temperamental traits are all something in an individual's character that makes the stock market an unsuitable investment alternative for the particular individual.

Just as some individuals are not suited for the mental demands of the stock market, some individuals are temperamentally unsuited for investing in limited partnerships. There is the ever-present risk of losing the entire investment made in any one limited partnerships. But beyond this, there is more. Unlike the stock market in which you can watch the daily swings, you are cut off from your investment in most limited partnerships. Generally, you make your investment and then have no control whatsoever over that investment until the general partner is ready to sell out the underlying assets of the partnership and liquidate. Not only have you no control over the investment, but you have no real way of influencing the management of your investment. Some individuals just are not suited temperamentally to abandon all control over their investments in this fashion. If you cannot accept the increased risk of a limited partnership and are uncomfortable with giving up all control over your investment for the necessary length of time, you should concentrate on investments other than limited partnerships.

Sizing Up the Investments

In Chapter 7, we considered methods of evaluating limited partnerships as to potential return and ways to compare limited partnership returns to alternative investments. But the numbers arrived at are only as good as the assumptions and projections underlying the calculations. How comfortable we are with the assumptions and projections, in other words, the degree to which we are willing to rely on them, is much more a matter of subjective analysis of the particular limited partnership and its sponsor or general partner. In attempting to come to grips with the more subjective aspects of evaluating a limited partnership investment, the place to begin is with the offering material, the prospectus and limited partnership agreement.

It is from this material that you will learn the basic structure of the partnership program. You will learn what benefits are being offered and what type of return to expect. The offering materials are a good starting point for forming an idea of the capabilities of the general partner and its management team, those to whom, if you invest, you will be entrusting your hard-earned dollars, generally with no chance to second guess your decision once you have made the investment.

Of course, the underlying investments that will be made by the partnership, such as real estate, oil and gas, equipment, trailer parks, adult congregate living centers, and so forth, are very important in reaching your decision as to whether to invest in a particular program or not. You have to be satisfied that the economic prospects for the underlying investments are good before deciding to invest. For this, I leave you to other works covering the specific assets involved as well as current economic analyses. Keep in mind that this is as much a part of your limited partnership research as studying the structure of the program and the competency of the general partner. If you are considering real estate partnerships, learn as much as you can about real estate before investing. The same applies to oil and gas, equipment leasing, or any other assets that may serve as the underlying investment for a limited partnership program.

GENERAL PARTNER'S TRACK RECORD

Whether a particular limited partnership will deliver the promised benefits depends to a great extent on the capabilities of the partnership's general partner. Look at the track record of the general partner, that is, the general partner's history of successes or failures in previous investment activities. Is it a good one? A good record is one that reflects success in a number of prior programs, not just averages.

One spectacular success can hide numerous failures or mediocre results in averages.

If the general partner's track record is good, look beyond this and try to determine if the management people that were involved with the prior successes are the same people that will be managing the particular limited partnership that you are considering. A change in management very well might presage a change in results. Still another point to explore in connection with the general partner's track record is the type of limited partnership programs in which the prior successes were scored. Just as with a change in management people, a change in the type of program undertaken can mean results will be less than those achieved in prior programs. Individuals competent to manage, for example, commercial or industrial property, are not necessarily competent to manage residential real estate or operate hotel and resort properties.

GENERAL PARTNER'S COMPENSATION

Another consideration you definitely will want to explore in sizing up a particular limited partnership is the way in which the general partner is compensated for its efforts. The question you want to ask and answer is: Does the general partner's compensation depend on his performance, or does all his profit depend on fees? The general partner of a limited partnership usually receives compensation in two forms: (1) fees, both for initiating the partnership and managing the underlying assets of the partnership, and (2) a share, that is, a participation in the results of the investment. In many cases today, the front-end costs of a limited partnership, the up-front fees going to the general partner, are kept low to attract investors. Low front-end costs, however, do not necessarily provide an advantage for limited partner investors if the general partner takes out too much down the road.

Obviously, almost every limited partnership is going to be structured so that the general partner or sponsor profits to some extent, even if the limited partnership ultimately fails. What you want to do is to satisfy yourself that the general partner is not too greedy in the way it has structured its compensation package at the expense of your chance to profit. There are a couple of rating services that do rate limited partnerships as to the "fairness" of the general partner's compensation in relation to what is offered to investors. These are mentioned in a later section in connection with the discussion of the problems associated with rating limited partnerships in the same way stocks and bonds are rated.

In assessing the general partner's compensation, or looking at the compensation ratings of others, keep in mind that the more important question, the ultimate question, if you will, is whether the general partner is any good. Some general partners simply may not be worth the cost of their compensation no matter how generous their compensation package is toward investors. After all, if the general partner fails to deliver on the potential of the investment, the limited partners get nothing. On the other hand, a general partner that delivers spectacular results for limited partners is worth every cent of its compensation. Look at the structure of the limited partnership – the general partner's compensation arrangements and possible conflicts of interest arising from them – but look even harder at the general partner's record on delivering results for its limited partners.

Other points to check with regard to the general partner include whether or not the general partner (or its parent company) is itself investing in the partnership and how solvent the general partner is. If the general partner is not backing the limited partnership with its own assets, you might want to ask why not. Also check out the possible conflicts of interest between the general partner and the limited partnership's operations and assets. Consider whether any conflicts might have a serious effect on the performance of the general partner in the management of the limited partnership.

In short, before investing in a limited partnership, you want to assure yourself that what you are purchasing is the investment that is being "sold" to you. If you can't satisfy yourself that a particular limited partnership and its general partner are as advertised, look for an alternative investment.

WHAT DOES YOUR BROKER HAVE TO GAIN?

When a broker or a financial planner sells you a financial product, he naturally earns a commission. In the usual case, if you purchase stocks or bonds from a broker, you receive a statement that separately itemizes the commission you are charged. This is not necessarily the case if you purchase a limited partnership interest.

Keep in mind that while some financial planners do not sell products as part of their service, most do. In a study released by the SEC in early 1988, the SEC staff reported that 85 percent of the inspected planners sold financial products, but only 47 percent informed prospective clients of this. The SEC study was based on field inspections of financial planners' records, academic studies, and surveys by private organizations. The report also disclosed that of those financial planning organizations that sell products, 81 percent sell real estate limited partnerships.

In any event, your broker or financial planner generally has more to gain by selling you a limited partnership interest than some other investment product. For the most part, commissions on limited partnerships are higher, usually in the 6 percent to 10 percent range, than other investment products. For instance, the commission on a common stock purchase of the same magnitude might be in the 2 percent to 3 percent range, although the commissions may rise to as much as 10 percent on a new issue. Bond purchases generally result in commissions of less than 6 percent.

If you purchase a limited partnership interest, you are not likely to see the commissions reflected on any receipt or confirmation slip. You will, however, find the commissions paid to brokers and other sellers of partnership units listed in the prospectus. In the simplest of terms, if the partnership pays sellers 10 percent of your investment dollar, you have 10 percent less working for you in the partnership than your investment would otherwise indicate. A $5,000 investment in a partnership unit with a 10 percent commission means that you have only $4,500 working for you in the partnership. This is not necessarily bad, it's just something you should be aware of and take into account if you are offered a limited partnership investment opportunity.

A more recent development in the limited partnership area is the emergence of "no-load" limited partnerships. These public partnership programs are offered to the general public directly by the general partner or sponsor of the program, usually through direct mail. Like their counterparts in the mutual fund industry, no-load investments are not necessarily better or worse than those sold through brokers or other intermediaries with a sales charge or commission. If you are interested in limited partnerships as an investment alternative, you should explore both types of offerings.

RATING LIMITED PARTNERSHIPS

The more or less subjective aspects of evaluating limited partnerships has been a stumbling block in developing a rating system similar to the bond ratings that are familiar to investors. There are at least two companies that presently rate limited partnerships, but their ratings are limited in scope and do not provide an overall assessment of the likely performance of the rated partnership. Standard & Poor's, a leading bond rating agency, is working on a partnership rating system that someday may provide a bit more guidance. In the meantime, investors, for the most part, must rely on their own evaluations of a limited partnership, as gleaned from the prospectus and the limited amount of available additional information.

There are a number of newsletters that review new limited partnership offerings. Those newsletters that do look at specific offerings, however, generally review only a few offerings per issue. Other newsletters restrict their coverage of limited partnerships to general industry-wide analyses and do not examine specific partnership offerings at all. In addition to these newsletters, some of the major brokerage houses follow master limited partnerships that are listed on the exchanges, but these limited partnerships make up only a small percentage of all public limited partnerships.

The two firms that currently rate limited partnerships are Robert A. Stanger & Co. and Southport Advisors Inc. Of the two, Stanger is probably the more widely known. Stanger offers two ratings, a risk rating and an offering terms rating. The risk ratings cover real estate and oil and gas limited partnerships, while the offering terms ratings extend to leasing and cable TV partnerships in addition to real estate and oil and gas. The risk rating is based on the type of the underlying investment of the partnership rather than on the specific offering. Accordingly, a limited partnership that will purchase existing commercial property with tenants already in place and current cash flow will receive a better risk rating than a limited partnership that will develop new residential property.

The more widely followed rating offered by Stanger is its offering terms rating. Again, this rating does not rate the entire partnership, nor is it designed to provide an assessment of the likely overall performance of the partnership. The offering terms rating is merely an assessment of the limited partnership's compensation arrangement, that is, how much the sponsor or general partner is taking out of the program in relation to the investors. The rating carries no indication of the general partner's abilities, past performance, or future prospects.

Southport Advisors lists all current partnerships and also gives two ratings. Its risk rating ranks partnerships according to their relative risks in relation to other investments and each other based on a scale from I to V. The lowest risk rating, I, is given to money market instru-

Sample Limited Partnership Agreement
with Annotations

The following is a sample of a limited partnership agreement. It is based on the agreement actually used for a diversified public real estate limited partnership. The agreement has been edited to eliminate much of the "boiler plate" and to provide comments to aid your understanding of these agreements. A review of this agreement should help you pinpoint important provisions in the partnership agreement for a limited partnership that you may be considering as an investment alternative. You will find the partnership agreement for a public limited partnership offering that you may be considering set out in full in the prospectus for that offering.

Outline of Agreement

This AGREEMENT OF LIMITED PARTNERSHIP is entered into by and among Sponsor Corporation, as General Partner, and Any Individual, as the Initial Limited Partner, together with the persons who become General Partners and Limited Partners of the Fund, as provided herein. The Fund was formed by the filing with the Secretary of State of the State of Delaware of a certificate of limited partnership. All capitalized terms used herein have the meanings set forth in Article II hereof.

ARTICLE I
ORGANIZATIONAL MATTERS

1.1 *Formation.* The General Partner and the Initial Limited Partner have formed the Fund as a limited partnership pursuant to the provisions of the Delaware Act. Except as expressly provided herein to the contrary, the rights and obligations of the Partners and the administration and termination of the Fund shall be governed by the Delaware Act. A Partnership Interest shall be personal property for all purposes.

Explanation: [As the definition in Article II tells us, the Delaware law involved is that state's version of the Revised Uniform Limited Partnership Act.]

1.2 *Name.* The name of the Fund shall be .... The Fund's business may be conducted under the name of the Fund or by any other name or names deemed advisable by the General Partner, including the name of the General Partner or any Affiliate thereof. The words or letters "Limited Partnership," "Ltd.," "L.P." or similar words or letters shall be included in the Fund's name where necessary for the purposes of complying with the laws of any jurisdiction that so requires. The General Partner in its sole discretion may change the name of the Fund at any time and from time to time upon 30-day's prior written notice to the other Partners.

1.3 *Registered Office; Principal Office.*

• • •

Explanation: [This provision contains the registered address in the state of formation for service of legal process, as well as the addresses from which the limited partnership's business is actually conducted.]

• • •

1.4 *Power of Attorney.*

(a) Each Limited Partner and each Assignee hereby irrevocably makes, constitutes and appoints the General Partner and the Liquidator (and any successor to either thereof by merger, assignment, election or otherwise) and each of their authorized officers and agents with full power of substitution as his true and lawful agent and attorney-in-fact, with full power and authority in his name, place and stead, to:

. . .

Explanation: [Contained here would be a long list of items that the limited partners agree to allow the general partner to execute on behalf of the limited partners, including the partnership agreement itself. This provision is necessary because of the large number of limited partners in a public limited partnership.]

. . .

Nothing herein contained shall be construed as authorizing the General Partner to amend this Agreement except in accordance with Article XIV or as may be otherwise expressly provided for in this Agreement.

(b) The foregoing power of attorney is hereby declared to be irrevocable and a special power of attorney coupled with an interest, and it shall survive and not be affected by the subsequent death, incompetency, disability, incapacity, dissolution, bankruptcy, insolvency or termination of any Limited Partner or Assignee and the transfer of all or any portion of his Partnership Interest and shall extend to such Limited Partner's or Assignee's heirs, successors, assigns and personal representatives. The foregoing power of attorney may be exercised by the General Partner or Liquidator on behalf of each Limited Partner and Assignee by a facsimile signature or by listing all of the Limited Partners and Assignees executing any instrument with a signature as attorney-in-fact for all of them. Each such Limited Partner and Assignee hereby agrees to be bound by any representations made by the General Partner or the Liquidator, acting in good faith pursuant to such power of attorney; and each such Limited Partner and Assignee hereby waives any and all defenses which may be available to contest, negate or disaffirm the action of the General Partner or the Liquidator, taken in good faith under such power of attorney.

Each Limited Partner and Assignee shall execute and deliver to the General Partner or the Liquidator, within 15 days after receipt of the General Partner's or the Liquidator's request therefor, such further designations, powers of attorney and other instruments as the General Partner or the Liquidator deems necessary to effectuate this Agreement and the purposes of the Fund.

1.5 *Term.* The Fund shall continue in existence until the close of Fund business on December 31, 2008, or until the earlier termination of the Fund in accordance with the provisions of Article XIII.

Explanation: [The limited partnership, with fixed termination date, avoids the corporate characteristic of continuity of life.]

ARTICLE II
DEFINITIONS

The following terms used in this Agreement shall have the following meanings unless otherwise expressly provided herein or unless the context otherwise requires.

• • •

"Adjusted Capital Contribution" means the Capital Contribution paid for or attributable to an Interest, reduced by the amount of any Capital Contributions which are not utilized to make real property investments and are returned to Interestholders and by the total of cash distributed from Sale or Refinancing Proceeds and from working capital reserves (to the extent such reserves come from Net Proceeds or Sale or Refinancing Proceeds) to the owner of such Interest and to all prior holders of such Interest. Adjusted Capital Contributions shall not be reduced by distributions of Cash Available for Distribution.

• • •

"Assignee" means any person who has been assigned a beneficial interest in an Interest, which assignment has been recorded on the books of the Fund, but who has not become a substituted Limited Partner.

• • •

"Capital Account" means the capital account maintained for a Partner or Assignee pursuant to Section 5.1

"Capital Contribution" means any cash, cash equivalents or Contributed Property which a Partner contributes to the Fund pursuant to Sections 4.1, 4.2 or 4.3. In the case of Interests sold pursuant to the Registration Statement, "Capital Contribution" means $1,000 with respect to each Interest purchased by a Limited Partner, which amount shall be attributed to such Interests in the hands of a subsequent Limited Partner or Assignee.

"Carrying Value" means (a) with respect to a Contributed Property, the Agreed Value of such property reduced (but not below zero) by all depreciation and cost recovery deductions charged to the Capital Accounts with respect to such property, and (b) with respect to any other property, the adjusted basis of such property for federal income tax purposes, as of the time of determination. The Carrying Value of any property shall be adjusted from time to time to the extent required by Sections 5.1(d) and 5.1(e), and to reflect changes, additions or other adjustments to the Carrying Value for dispositions, acquisitions or improvements of the Fund's properties, as deemed appropriate by the General Partner.

"Cash Available for Distribution" means the excess of cash revenues from Fund operations and earnings on Fund investments, if any, over cash expenditures (including the General Partner's partnership management fee, debt service and other payments to lenders, if any, and contributions, advances or cash set aside for improvements, expansion and renovation of properties), less allowances for working capital and other cash reserves as determined by the General Partner. Cash Available for Distribution does not include Sale or Refinancing Proceeds.

"Cash Flow from Operations" means Cash Available for Distribution before payment of the General Partner's partnership management fee and allowances for working capital and other cash reserves.

"Closing Date" means any date on which purchasers of Interests are admitted to the Fund as Limited Partners.

"Code" means the Internal Revenue Code of 1986, as amended and in effect from time to time, and applicable regulations thereunder. Any reference to a specific section or sections of the Code shall be deemed to include any corresponding provisions of future law.

• • •

"Delaware Act" means the Delaware Revised Uniform Limited Partnership Act, 6 Del. C. § 17-101, et seq., as it may be amended from time to time, and any successor to such Act.

• • •

"Front-End Fees" means fees and expenses paid by any party for any service rendered in connection with and during the Fund's organization and acquisition stages, including Organization and Offering Expenses, Acquisition Expenses, Acquisition Fees, Investigatory Fees, and any other similar fees, but excluding any development fee paid to a non-Affiliate of the General Partner (including any seller or any Affiliate of a seller and any unaffiliated joint venturer of the Fund) in connection with the actual development of a property after acquisition by the Fund.

• • •

"Gain From Sale" means any income or gain of the Fund for federal income tax purposes resulting from a Sale, except that if the Carrying Value of any asset differs from its adjusted basis for federal income tax purposes at the beginning of the taxable year, such income or gain will be calculated by reference to such Carrying Value.

• • •

"Interest" means a limited partnership interest in the Fund, which, in the case of Interests sold pursuant to the Registration Statement, shall represent a Capital Contribution to the Fund of $1,000.

"Interestholder" means the Limited Partner or Assignee in whose name an Interest is registered on the books of the Fund.

• • •

"Limited Partners" means the Initial Limited Partner and the other persons or entities who from time to time are admitted to the Fund and shown on the books of the fund as additional or substituted Limited Partners.

"Liquidator" means the person or entity approved pursuant to Section 13.3 who performs the functions described therein.

"Loss From Sale" means any net loss of the Fund for federal income tax purposes resulting from a Sale, except that if the Carrying Value of any asset differs from its adjusted basis at the beginning of its taxable year, such loss will be calculated by reference to such Carrying Value.

"Majority Vote" means the vote or approval of Limited Partners who beneficially own more than 50% of the Interests then Outstanding.

• • •

"Net Proceeds" means the total Gross Proceeds less Organization and Offering Expenses paid by the Fund.

"Nonaccountable Expense Allowance" means the amount payable to the General Partner pursuant to Section 7.2.

"Operating Cash Expenses" means, with respect to any fiscal period, the amount of cash disbursed in that period in the ordinary course of business during the period, including, without limitation, all operating expenses such as advertising and promotional, management, salary, utility, repair and maintenance, accounting, legal, statistical, or bookkeeping services, computing or accounting equipment use, travel and telephone expenses, and salaries and direct expenses of employees of the Fund, the General Partner and its Affiliates while engaged in Fund business. Operating Cash Expenses shall not include expenditures paid out of working capital reserves.

• • •

"Partners" means the General Partner and the Limited Partners, collectively, and "Partner" means any one of the Partners.

. . .

"Preferred Return" means an amount equal to 6% per annum on a Limited Partner's Adjusted Capital Contribution determined on a cumulative, noncompounded basis commencing on the first day of the first full calendar quarter after the Termination Date, and ending on the date as of which such amount is computed, such amount to be satisfied from Cash Available for Distribution and Sale or Refinancing Proceeds.

. . .

"Priority Return" means an amount equal to the difference between (a) an amount equal to 12% per annum on a Limited Partner's Adjusted Capital Contribution determined on a cumulative, noncompounded basis commencing on the first day of the first full calendar quarter after the Termination Date, and ending on the date as of which such amount is computed, and (b) the Preferred Return, such difference to be satisfied from Cash Available for Distribution and Sale or Refinancing Proceeds.

. . .

"Sale" means any of the following transactions of the Fund: sales, exchanges or other dispositions of real or personal property, condemnations, recoveries of damage awards and insurance proceeds (other than business or rental interruption insurance proceeds). The disposition of Fund property by transfer back to the seller or an Affiliate, whether in the form of a rescission, exchange or resale, or pursuant to an option or other similar arrangement entered into at or prior to the time of taking title to the property, shall not, if the proceeds from such transfer back are reinvested in another property, constitute a sale or disposition and shall not result in Sale or Refinancing Proceeds.

"Sale or Refinancing Proceeds" means the net cash received by the Fund from or as a result of a Sale or Refinancing of any property of the fund after deducting all expenses (including real estate commissions) relating to the transaction and amounts applied by the General Partner in its sole discretion toward the payment of indebtedness of the Fund. Sale or Refinancing Proceeds do not include proceeds of a Sale or Refinancing during the offering period. If the proceeds of any Sale or Refinancing for purposes of this definition.

"Substantially All of the Assets" means, unless the context otherwise requires, properties and other assets representing 66-2/3% or more of the original purchase price of the Fund's assets as of the end of the most recent calendar quarter.

. . .

ARTICLE III
PURPOSE

The purpose and business of the Fund shall be any business which may lawfully be conducted by a limited partnership organized pursuant to the Delaware Act, including primarily, but without limitation, the construction, development, acquisition, ownership, management, operation, leasing and disposition of the real properties, multifamily residential properties and other similar properties; the carrying on of any business relating thereto or arising therefrom; the entering into of any partnership, joint venture or other similar arrangement to engage in any of the foregoing or the ownership of interests in any entity engaged in any of the foregoing; and anything incidental or necessary to the foregoing. The Fund is not limited in the geographical area where it may conduct operations.

Explanation: [This is a broad purpose clause and gives the general partner wide discretion in changing the investment mix of the partnership as conditions warrant.]

ARTICLE IV
CAPITAL CONTRIBUTIONS

4.1 *General Partner*. The General Partner has contributed $1,000 in cash to the Fund on the date of this Agreement. On or before the first date on which its contributions could be required pursuant to the last sentence of Section 13.3, the General Partner shall contribute to the Fund cash or cash equivalents in the amount required pursuant to said last sentence of Section 13.3.

Explanation: [The general partner itself is not investing in the limited partnership, except to the extent of the $1,000. On liquidation, the general partner agrees to make up a deficit in its capital account because of losses suffered by the partnership, but this amount is limited to about 1 percent of the investments made by the limited partners.]

4.2 *Initial Limited Partner and Initial Public Offering.*

(a) The Initial Limited Partner has contributed $5,000 to the capital of the Fund and has received 5 Interests for such contribution.

(b) The General Partner is hereby authorized to raise capital for the Fund by purchasing for itself and by offering and selling to the public in an initial public offering on behalf of the Fund of up to 100,000 Interests (in addition to the Interests issued to the Initial Limited Partner pursuant to paragraph (a) above) and by admitting the purchasers of such Interests as Limited Partners of the Fund in the manner discussed below.

• • •

Explanation: [The mechanics of handling subscriptions and refunds in the event the minimum amount is not raised from investors are omitted.]

• • •

4.3 *Offering of Additional Interests.* The General Partner is hereby further authorized to offer and sell to the public up to 50,000 Interests in addition to those referred to in Section 4.2(b) above on or before one year after the effective date of the Registration Statement and to admit to the Fund, from time to time, one or more additional Limited Partners (including one or more existing Limited Partners who make additional Capital Contributions).

4.4 *Terms of Offering and Authority.* Except as otherwise provided in Sections 4.2 and 4.3, the General Partner shall have sole and complete discretion in determining the terms and conditions of the public offerings and sales of Interests...

4.5 *No Preemptive Rights.* No Partner or Assignee shall have any preemptive right...

4.6 *Interest.* No interest shall be paid by the Fund on Capital Contributions or on balances in Partners' or Assignees' Capital Accounts.

4.7 *No Withdrawal.* A Partner or Assignee shall not be entitled to withdraw any part of his or his predecessor's Capital Contribution or his Capital Account or to receive any distribution from the Fund, except as provided in Section 5.4, and Articles VII, XII and XIII.

Explanation: [The agreement provides for no guaranteed payments to partners based on their investments without regard to partnership income and gives limited partners no rights to demand a return of their investments.]

4.8 *Loans from Partners.* Loans by a Partner or Assignee to the Fund shall not be considered Capital Contributions.

• • •

ARTICLE V
ALLOCATIONS AND DISTRIBUTIONS

5.1 Maintenance of Capital Accounts.

(a) The Fund shall maintain for each Partner and Assignee a separate Capital Account in accordance with the rules of Treasury Regulation Section 1.704-1(b)(2)(iv).

· · ·

Explanation: [Capital accounts for partners that reflect each partner's adjusted investment in the partnership at any given time are maintained in conformity with the regulations issued by the Internal Revenue Service. The details are omitted. Essentially, the partnership is attempting to assure that all allocations to partners will have substantial economic effect and will be respected for tax purposes. See the discussion of special allocations in Chapter 4.]

· · ·

5.2 Allocation of Profits and Losses Generally. For purposes of maintaining the Capital Accounts and in determining the rights of the Partners and Assignees among themselves, except as provided in Sections 5.3 and 5.5 below, every item of Fund income, gain, loss, deduction and credit shall be allocated as follows:

(a) Except as otherwise provided in this Section 5.2 or in Sections 5.3 or 5.5, every item of Fund income, gain, loss, deduction and credit shall be allocated 99% to the Interestholders (in accordance with their Proportionate Shares) and 1% to the General Partner.

· · ·

Explanation: [This is the general profit and loss sharing ratio of this partnership. Again, lengthy provisions designed to comply with income tax regulations on substantial economic effect are omitted.]

· · ·

(c) Except as may be required by Section 13.3 in connection with winding up the Fund, a deficit may be carried in the Capital Account of the General Partner without the General Partner being required to make a contribution to the capital of the Fund, unless such contribution is necessary in order to meet obligations to creditors of the Fund other than Partners as such.

• • •

(e) Notwithstanding any other provision of this Agreement to the contrary, the interest of the General Partner in each material item of Fund income, gain, loss, deduction or credit shall be equal to at least 1% of each such item at all times during the existence of the Fund. In determining the General Partner's interest in such item, Interests owned by the General Partner shall not be taken into account.

5.3 *Allocation of Gain or Loss from Sale.* For purposes of maintaining the Capital Accounts and in determining the rights of the Partners and Assignees among themselves, Gain From Sale and Loss From Sale shall be allocated as follows:

Explanation: [Gain or loss from sales of partnership property are allocated according to the special allocation provisions contained in this section. Note that if the partnership is profitable, 20 percent of the gain goes to the general partner and 80 percent to limited partners, compared to the 1 percent to 99 percent split for operating income. However, the order of distribution spelled out below (Section 5.4) requires limited partners to receive 12 percent on their capital contributions before distribution of sale proceeds, other than commissions, can be made to the general partner. This does give the limited partners a return before the general partner begins taking its share, at least as to gains on property prior to liquidation of the partnership.]

(a) To the extent that the Capital Accounts of the Interestholders are negative, Gain From Sale shall first be allocated 99% to the Capital Accounts of such Interestholders and 1% to the Capital Account of the General Partner in proportion to such negative Capital Accounts until the Capital Accounts of such Interestholders equal zero;

(b) To the extent that the General Partner has any remaining negative balance in its Capital Account, Gain From Sale shall next be allocated to the Capital Account of the General Partner to the extent of such negative Capital Account;

(c) Gain From Sale shall next be allocated to the Capital Accounts of Interestholders to the extent necessary to make the aggregate balance thereof equal to the Adjusted Capital Contributions with respect to the Interests then held by such Interestholders in proportion to such Adjusted Capital Contributions;

(d) Gain From Sale shall next be allocated to the Capital Accounts of the Interestholders to the extent necessary to make the aggregate balance therein equal to the sum of (i) the Interestholders' Adjusted Capital Contributions and (ii) any deficiency in the Preferred Return of the Interestholders;

(e) Gain From Sale shall next be allocated to the Interestholders in an amount sufficient to make the aggregate balance in their Capital Accounts equal to the sum of (i) their Adjusted Capital Contributions, (ii) any deficiency in their Preferred Return and (iii) and deficiency in their Priority Return;

(f) Gain From Sale shall next be allocated to the General Partner in an amount sufficient to bring the balance of its Capital Account to an amount equal to 25% of any deficiency in the Priority Return of the Interestholders allocated pursuant to paragraph (e); and

(g) The balance of any Gain From Sale shall next be allocated 20% to the General Partner and 80% to the Interestholders in accordance with their Percentage Interests.

(h) Loss From Sale shall be allocated 99% to the Capital Accounts of the Interestholders and 1% to the Capital Account of the General Partner; provided, however, if any such allocation of loss would reduce any Interestholder's Capital Account below zero or would increase the negative balance in such Interestholder's Capital Account at a time when another Interestholder has a positive Capital Account, determined (i) after taking into account the reduction of any negative balance in such Capital Account in accordance with Section 5.1(c), (ii) after taking into account all prior or contemporaneous cash distributions and all prior or contemporaneous allocations of income, gain, loss, deduction or credit and (iii) as determined at the close of the taxable year in respect of which such loss is to be allocated, such excess losses shall be allocated to those Interestholders with a positive Capital Account in proportion to such positive Capital Accounts until no Interestholder shall have a positive Capital Account; any remaining losses shall be allocated to the General Partner.

(i) Notwithstanding anything in this Section 5.3 to the contrary, the General Partner may allocate Gain From Sale among the Partners and Assignees so that the Capital Account balances of each Partner and Assignee upon dissolution of the Fund shall be as close as possible to the amount of cash such Partner and Assignee would receive if the proceeds to be distributed pursuant to Section 5.4(c) were distributed pursuant to Section 5.4(b).

5.4 *Order of Distribution*. Distributions shall be made in accordance with the following:

Explanation: [Since the partnership is a conduit, allocations of income, loss, etc., as spelled out in the preceding section, must be made regardless of actual cash distributions. This provision now spells out the priority of any actual distributions if the general partner decides to make a distribution. Note that the general partner is not required to make actual distributions, and whether to make distributions or not is usually a matter of the general partner's discretion.]

(a) Any distribution of Cash Available for Distribution, including all amounts attributable thereto, shall be made to the General Partner and Interestholders in accordance with their Percentage Interests.

(b) Distribution of Sale or Refinancing Proceeds, including all amounts attributable thereto (other than upon the dissolution of the Fund) shall be made as follows:

(i) first, to the Interestholders in an amount equal to their Adjusted Capital Contributions, in proportion to such Adjusted Capital Contributions;

(ii) second, to the Interestholders in an amount equal to any deficiency in their Preferred Return;

(iii) third, to the General Partner in an amount equal to any unpaid real estate sales commissions then due the General Partner or its Affiliates;

(iv) fourth, to the Interestholders in an amount equal to any deficiency in their Priority Return;

(v) fifth, to the General Partner in an amount equal to 25% of the aggregate amount (on a cumulative basis), if any, paid to the Interestholders pursuant to paragraph (iv) above; and

(vi) the balance, if any, 80% to the Interestholders and 20% to the General Partner.

(c) Subject to the provisions of Section 13.3, any distribution upon dissolution of the Fund shall be made as follows:

(i) first, to the Partners and Assignees having positive balances in their Capital Accounts after making allocations pursuant to Section 5.3, in an amount equal to such positive balances, in proportion to such positive balances; and

(ii) the balance, if any, to the Partners and Assignees in accordance with their Percentage Interests.

(d) Any distribution of funds available for distribution shall be made or not made in the sole discretion of the General Partner. To the extent the General Partner elects to distribute amounts held in any reserve fund to Partners and Assignees, such amounts shall be distributed in the manner they would have been distributed if such funds had not been placed in the reserve fund, but originally distributed as provided in this Section 5.4.

5.5 Persons Entitled to Allocations and Distributions.

(a) If any Interest is transferred during any fiscal quarter of the Fund every item of Fund income, gain, loss, deduction and credit attributable to such Interest for the fiscal year shall be divided and allocated between the transferor and the transferee based upon a convention selected by the General Partner, in its sole discretion. Distributions shall be made to the Record Holder of the Interest as of the Record Date.

(b) With respect to any period during which an Interestholder is first entitled to a share of Fund income, gain, loss, deduction or credit, the Fund shall, with respect to such items of income, gain, loss, deduction or credit, allocate such items among the persons who are entitled to such items on a basis consistent with the provisions of the Code and the regulations promulgated thereunder.

(c) Notwithstanding the provisions of this Article V, prior to the Initial Closing Date, all allocations of income, gain, loss, deduction and credit and distributions shall be allocated and distributed 20% to the General Partner and 80% to the Initial Limited Partner.

5.6 *Tax Allocations.*

(a) Except as otherwise provided in this Section 5.6, allocations of income, gain, loss, and deduction and credit for federal income tax purposes shall be made in accordance with Sections 5.2, 5.3 and 5.5.

• • •

Explanation: [Tax allocations generally follow allocations spelled out above and are designed to have substantial economic effect so that they are respected for tax purposes by the Internal Revenue Service. The general partner is given the power to alter allocation provisions to assure that they conform to the income tax regulations dealing with substantial economic effect.]

• • •

(d) It is intended that the allocations prescribed in Sections 5.3, 5.5 and 5.6 will constitute allocations for federal income tax purposes that are consistent with Section 704 of the Code and will comply with any limitations or restrictions therein, to the extent reasonably possible without causing Interests to lack uniform characteristics for federal income tax purposes. To preserve uniformity of Interests, the General Partner shall have sole discretion to (i) adopt such conventions as it deems appropriate in determining the amount of depreciation and cost recovery deductions; (ii) make special allocations of income or deduction; and (iii) amend the provisions of this Agreement as appropriate (a) to reflect the proposal or promulgation of Treasury Regulations under Section 704(c) of the Code, or (b) otherwise to preserve the uniformity of Interests issued or sold from time to time. The General Partner may adopt such conventions, make such allocations and make such amendments to this Agreement as provided in this Section 5.6(d) without the approval of the Interestholders only if they would not have a material adverse effect on the Interestholders as a group and if such allocations are consistent with, and supportable under, the principles of Section 704 of the Code.

5.7 *Certain Payments Not Distributions.* Any amounts paid pursuant to Article VII shall not be deemed to be distributions for purposes of this Agreement.

5.8 *Special Allocations.* If any fees deducted for federal income tax purposes by the Fund are recharacterized by a final determination by the Internal Revenue Service as nondeductible distributions to a General Partner, then notwithstanding all other allocation provisions herein, gross income shall be allocated to the General Partner (for the year(s) of adjustment) in an amount equal to such recharacterized fees. Any loss or deductions attributable to such recharacterized fees shall be allocated to the General Partner as such time and in such manner as permitted by the Code.

ARTICLE VI
MANAGEMENT AND OPERATION OF THE FUND

6.1 *Management of the Fund; Authority of the General Partner.* The General Partner shall have exclusive authority to manage the operations and affairs of the Fund and to make all decisions regarding the business of the Fund. Pursuant to the foregoing, it is understood and agreed that the General Partner shall have all the rights and powers of a general partner as provided in the Delaware Act (or any successor act) and as otherwise provided by law and this Agreement, and any action taken by the General Partner shall constitute the act of and serve to bind the Fund. The General Partner shall, except as otherwise provided by this Agreement or the Delaware Act, have all the rights and powers and be subject to all restrictions and liabilities of a partner in a partnership without limited partners. In dealing with the General Partner acting on behalf of the fund, no purchaser, seller, lender or any other person or entity dealing with the Fund shall be required to inquire into the authority of the General Partner to bind the Fund and shall be entitled to rely exclusively on the representations of the General Partner as to its power and authority to act on behalf of the Fund and to enter into any purchase, sale, financing or other transaction on behalf of the Fund.

Explanation: [The general partner is given broad powers to manage the partnership and its assets and to conduct the business affairs of the partnership.]

6.2 *Responsibilities of the General Partner.* Without otherwise limiting the rights or powers of the General Partner, the General Partner shall only be responsible for the following services to the Fund:

(a) supervising the organization of the Fund and the offering and sale of Interests;

(b) arranging for (i) the identification of properties and other investments suitable for the Fund; (ii) a review of the significant factors in deciding whether or not to invest in a particular property or investment; and (iii) if a decision is made to make a particular investment, the making of such investment;

(c) the performance and supervision of Fund management, which includes: (i) establishing policies for the operation of the Fund; (ii) causing the Fund's agents or employees to arrange for the provision of services necessary to the operation of the Fund (including, without limitation, property management, investor, accounting and legal services and services relating to distributions by the Fund); (iii) when necessary or appropriate, approving actions to be taken by the Fund; (iv) providing advice, consultation, analysis and supervision with respect to the functions of the Fund as an owner of Fund properties (including, without limitation, decisions regarding the terms and conditions of material leases affecting Fund properties, decisions regarding material adjustments to rental schedules, the sale, disposition or refinancing of Fund properties and compliance with federal, state and local regulatory requirements and procedures); (v) executing documents on behalf of the Fund; and (vi) making all decisions as to accounting and tax matters; and

(d) approving of the terms of any borrowings and the sale, disposition or refinancing of Fund properties, including establishing the terms for and arranging any such transaction.

6.3 *Rights and Powers of the General Partner.* In addition to the authority otherwise granted by the Delaware Act and elsewhere in this Agreement, General Partner is hereby granted all rights, powers and authority to do on behalf of the Fund all things deemed necessary, proper or desirable by it, in its sole discretion to conduct the business and affairs of the Fund, including, but not limited to, and subject only to such limitations and/or approvals set forth in this Agreement, the right, power and authority:

(a) to acquire, improve, hold and dispose of real property (including properties which are recently completed, under construction or under contract for development and properties which may require refurbishing or additional leasing activity), interests-therein, portions thereof or appurtenances thereto, as well as personal or mixed property connected therewith, including the purchase, construction, alteration, repairing, razing, replacing, rebuilding, improvement, maintenance, exchange, trade or sale of such properties, at such price or amount, for cash, securities (in compliance with appropriate securities regulations) or other property, including mortgages, and upon terms, as the General Partner deems, in its sole discretion, to be in the best interests of the Fund;

(b) to let or lease all or any portion of any property for any purpose and without limitation as to the term thereof, whether or not such term (including renewals) shall extend beyond the date of the termination of the Fund and whether or not the portion so leased is to be occupied by the lessee or, in turn, subleased in whole or in part to others, at such rental or amount and upon terms, as the General Partner deems, in its sole discretion, to be in the best interests of the Fund;

(c) to create, by grant or otherwise, easements and servitudes, and, subject to paragraphs(r) and (x)below and paragraphs (d), (v), (w) and (x) of Section 6.4, to cause the Fund to borrow money, guarantee, assume or contract for debt and, if security is required therefor, to mortgage or subject any Fund investment to any other security device, to obtain replacements of any mortgage or other security device, and to prepay, in whole or in part, refinance, recast, increase, modify, consolidate, extend or accept prepayment of, any mortgage or other security device, all of the foregoing on such terms and in such amounts as the General Partner, in its sole discretion, deems to be in the best interests of the Fund;

(d) to place record title to, or the right to use, Fund assets in the name(s) of nominee(s), trustee(s) or others for any purpose convenient or beneficial to the Fund;

(e) to acquire and enter into any contract of insurance which the General Partner deems necessary or appropriate for the protection of the Fund and the General Partner for the conservation of Fund assets, or for any purpose convenient or beneficial to the Fund;

(f) to employ and dismiss persons in the operation and management of the business of the Fund including, but not limited to, general contractors, independent contractors, architects, engineers, consultants, supervisory managing agents, building management agents, insurance brokers, real estate brokers, loan brokers, agents, managers, attorneys, accountants and others on such terms and for such compensation as the General Partner shall determine, provided, however, that (i) real estate brokerage commissions and similar fees paid in connection with the sale of a Fund property shall not exceed the limitations with respect thereto set forth in Section 7.6; (ii) agreements with the General Partner or its Affiliates for the services set forth in Article VII shall not be inconsistent with the terms and limitations as to fees and expenses set forth in Article VII; and (iii) in any contract with an independent contractor relating to the management or development of Fund properties, the General Partner shall use its best efforts to provide the authority to exercise overall supervision over the performance of such contracts, to terminate the independent contractor on such terms as the General Partner shall deem appropriate and to restructure such contracts so as to comply with exemptions from "plan asset" treatment set forth in regulations promulgated by the U.S. Department of Labor;

(g) to prepare or cause to be prepared reports, statements, and other relevant information for distribution to Interestholders, including annual and quarterly and other interim reports;

(h) to open accounts and deposit and maintain funds in the name of the Fund in banks or savings and loan associations, including money market and other accounts and certificates of deposit...;

(i) to cause the Fund to make or revoke any of the elections on behalf of the Fund, including, but not limited to, those referred to in Sections 108, 195, 709, 754, 856 or 1017 of the Code or any similar provision enacted in lieu thereof;

(j) to select as the Fund's accounting year the calendar year or such other fiscal year as approved by the Internal Revenue Service (the Fund shall operate on a fiscal year which ends December 31 unless the General Partner selects another annual accounting year, subject to approval by the Internal Revenue Service);

(k) to determine the appropriate accounting method or methods to be used by the Fund in maintaining its books and records;

(l) to offer and sell Interests in the Fund to the public directly or through any Affiliate of the General Partner licensed as a securities broker-dealer and to employ personnel, agents and dealers for such purpose;

(m) to require in all third party Fund obligations that the General Partner shall not have any personal liability thereon, but that the person or entity contracting with the Fund is to look solely to the Fund and its assets for satisfaction thereof and in the event that any such obligation provides for personal liability, the General Partner may require its satisfaction prior to contracts without such personal liability; provided, however, that the inclusion of the aforesaid provisions shall not materially affect the cost of the service or material being supplied and all Fund obligations are satisfied in accordance with prudent business practices as to time and manner of payment;

(n) to purchase properties in its own name or in the name of an Affiliate or nominee, a trust or a corporate "nominee" or otherwise and temporarily hold title thereto for the purpose of facilitating the acquisition of such property; provided that such property is purchased by the Fund for a purchase price no greater than the cost (including carrying costs of whatever nature) of such property to the General Partner or an Affiliate, except for compensation in accordance with Article VII of this Agreement;

(o) to invest the Gross Proceeds or Net proceeds temporarily, prior and subsequent to investment in properties, and to invest the Fund's working capital and other cash reserves, in United States government securities, certificates of deposit of United States banks, bank repurchase agreements covering securities of the United States government or governmental agencies, bankers' acceptances and commercial paper rated A-1 or better by Moody's Investors Service, Inc. and money market funds, and mutual funds investing in short and intermediate term debt securities within the three highest credit categories assigned by established rating agencies, or if not rated, of the equivalent investment quality as determined by the General Partner, and interest- bearing money market accounts, certificates of deposit and other time deposits in banks and thrift institutions, provided, however, that prior to receiving and accepting subscriptions for the minimum number of Interests as described in Section 4.2(b) hereof, the Gross Proceeds may be invested temporarily only in short-term United States government securities, securities issued or guaranteed by United States government agencies or certificates of deposit or time or demand deposits in commercial banks, or any other investments permitted by Rule 15c2-4 under the Securities Exchange Act of 1934, as amended. Funds invested with Affiliates must receive interest and/or dividends at a rate competitive with those available from similar unrelated financial institutions, and funds invested with an affiliated entity may not exceed 5% of the assets of that Affiliate. No compensating balance arrangements in connection with such investments will be permitted, other than those which may be provided to the Fund;

(p) to make expenditures on behalf of the Fund and to establish, maintain, increase and reduce cash reserves of the Fund; such reserves may be funded, in the discretion of the General Partner, from Net Proceeds, Cash Flow from Operations and Sale or Refinancing Proceeds and may be used for such purposes as the General Partner shall deem appropriate, including, but not limited to, normal repairs, replacements, capital and tenant improvements, contingencies, accruals, insurance, real estate taxes and related items, distributions to Partners and other Fund purposes. The General Partner shall initially endeavor to maintain a cash reserve in an amount equal to 1.5% of Gross Proceeds applicable to the acquisition of properties. Upon the sale of a property, any reserves applicable thereto may be applied to other properties. Any funds from reserves which are expended need not be restored and after the Net Proceeds have been fully or substantially invested and income and expense levels ascertained, the General

Partner may elect to reduce reserves, if deemed appropriate, to any amount not less than 1% of Gross Proceeds applicable to investments in properties then owned by the Fund;

(q) to sign checks or Fund certificates on behalf of the Fund;

(r) with respect to borrowings described in Sections 6.3(x), to allow the Fund to borrow money from the General Partner or its Affiliates on a short-term basis, at any time and from time to time, and in connection therewith to pay interest and other financing charges or fees which would be charged by unaffiliated third parties on comparable loans; provided however, that the interest rate charged on any such loan shall not exceed two percentage points over the prime lending rate and provided further that no prepayment charge or penalty shall be required by General Partner or Affiliates on any such loan to the Fund;

(s) to amend this Agreement from time to time pursuant to the authority granted by Sections 1.5, 5.1(f), 5.6(d), 6.3, 10.8, 12.6 and Article XIV hereof;

(t) to sign and deliver any certificate which any person dealing with the Fund or the General Partner may rely upon as authority with respect to: (a) the identity of any Partner or Assignee; (b) the existence or nonexistence of any fact or facts which constitute precedent to acts by any Partner or relating to any other matter germane to the affairs of the fund; (c) the persons who are authorized to execute and deliver any instrument or document of the Fund; or (d) any act or failure to act by the Fund or as to any other matter whatsoever involving the Fund or any Partner or Assignee;

(u) to form any further limited or general partnerships, joint ventures or other relationships, the purposes of which are consistent with the investment objectives and policies of the fund;

(v) to control any matters affecting the rights and obligations of the Fund, including the conduct of the litigation and the incurring of legal expenses and settlement of claims and litigation;

(w) to bring and defend actions at law or in equity and indemnify any person against liabilities and contingencies to the extent permitted by law and not prohibited by this Agreement;

(x) to borrow funds, for purpose of (i) funding the acquisition of properties prior to the availability of proceeds of the offering, (ii) financing capital expenditures, including refurbishments or repairs, or operating deficits, (iii) meeting working capital requirements, (iv) refinancing indebtedness incurred for the foregoing purposes, or (v) providing capital to the Fund at any time and for any purpose which the General Partner deems necessary taking into consideration the general policy of the Fund to avoid the incurrence of indebtedness;

(y) to execute, acknowledge and deliver any and all instruments to effectuate the rights and obligations set forth herein, and to take all such action in connection therewith as the General partner shall deem necessary or appropriate; and

(z) to take such other actions as are necessary, desirable or required in connection with the Fund's affairs to the extent permitted by law except as the same may be prohibited by the terms of this Agreement.

6.4 *General Policies of the Fund and Limitations on the Authority of the General Partner.* Neither the General Partner nor any Affiliate shall have the authority to:

Explanation: [Here is where the actual limits on the otherwise almost absolute power of the general partner are found. This section of the partnership agreement should be scrutinized carefully. Generally, if an act is not listed here, the general partner can do it, even if it is not listed among the specific grants of power set out above.]

(a) enter into service contracts with the fund which would bind the Fund after the effective date of the removal of the General Partner as general partner of the Fund;

(b) grant to it or any of its Affiliates an exclusive listing for the sale of Fund assets, including Fund properties;

(c) except upon the approval by a Majority Vote pursuant to Section 8.5(e), sell Substantially All of the Assets of the Fund in a single sale, or in multiple sales in the same 12-month period, except (i) sales in the ordinary course of business, (ii) the sale of the Fund's final property, (iii) sales of mortgage loans acquired in connection with the sale of the Fund's real properties and (iv) sales in the orderly liquidation and winding up of the business of the Fund upon its termination and dissolution in the ordinary course of its business;

(d) except upon the approval by a Majority Vote pursuant to Section 8.5(f), pledge or encumber Substantially All of the Assets of the Fund at one time;

(e) except upon the approval of a Majority Vote pursuant to Section 8.5(i), materially alter the nature of the business of the Fund as set forth in Article III or materially change the three principal investment objectives of the Fund as described in the prospectus contained in the Registration Statement;

(f) receive a rebate or give-up or participate in any reciprocal business arrangement which would enable it or an Affiliate to do so;

(g) cause the Fund to sell real or personal property to any entity in which the General Partner or any Affiliate thereof has an interest, other than a joint venture or similar program which complies with the conditions set forth in paragraph (h) below and unless the proceeds of the offering of Interests are insufficient to retain a property or properties acquired by the Fund, in which case such transfer shall be made for the amount of the Fund's cash payments therefor and the assumption of the obligations related thereto, provided such transfer is believed in good faith by the General Partner to be in the best interests of the Fund, taking into account its investment objectives and policies and financial position and the characteristics and suitability of the properties to be sold and maintained by the Fund;

(h) cause the Fund to invest in any program, partnership or other venture unless: (i) it is a general partnership, a joint venture or a tenancy in common; (ii) except as described below, the other partner or owner is not an Affiliate of the General Partner; (iii) such general partnership, joint venture or tenancy in common owns and operates a particular property and the Fund acquires the controlling interest in such entity; (iv) the Fund, as a result of the form of such ownership of a property, is not charged, directly or indirectly, more than once for the same service; (v) the agreement of partnership, joint venture or tenancy in common or other controlling agreement does not authorize the Fund to do anything as a partner, joint venturer, tenant in common or controlling person with respect to the property which the Fund, or the General Partner, could not do directly because of the policies set forth in this Agreement; and (vi) the General Partner and its Affiliates are prohibited from receiving any compensation, fee or expense which is not permitted to be paid under the terms of this Agreement. Notwithstanding the foregoing, the Fund shall be permitted to invest in joint venture arrangements with an Affiliate of the General Partner if all of the following conditions are met: (i) such Affiliate has investment objectives substantially identical to those of the Fund; (ii) there are no duplicate property management or other fees; (iii) the compensation payable to the general partner(s) or sponsor(s) of such Affiliate is substantially identical to that payable to the General Partner; (iv) each investor has a right of first refusal to buy out the interest of the other investor; and (v) the investment of the fund and the Affiliate in the joint venture is on substantially the same terms and conditions (although not necessarily the same percentages). Any investment pursuant to this subparagraph shall be made consistently with the then existing Securities and Exchange Commission interpretations and case law respecting the applicability of the Investment Company Act of 1940. Prior to the exercise of any right of first refusal, the General Partner or an Affiliate shall obtain an opinion of counsel or other reasonable assurance to (or satisfactory to) the General Partner that such exercise will not violate ERISA;

(i) except as permitted by this Agreement in Article VII and Section 6.3(n) and paragraph (g) or (h) above, purchase real or personal property from the Fund or sell or lease real or personal property to the Fund;

(j) cause the Fund to purchase any property without first having obtained an appraisal with respect to the value thereof, rendered by an independent appraiser who is a member of a nationally recognized society of appraisers, in which the appraised value supports the purchase price of such property (such appraisals shall be retained at the office of the Fund for at least five years and will be available for inspection and duplication by any Interestholder);

(k) cause the Fund to exchange Interests for real property;

(l) cause the Fund to borrow funds, except under the circumstances described in Section 6.3(x);

Explanation: [This partnership is not designed to be a leveraged investment, that is, acquisition of assets for the partnership generally will be funded entirely from investors' capital contributions. Limited borrowing power, however, is granted to the general partner.]

(m) cause the Fund to finance the purchase of real property, except in connection with acquisitions made prior to the availability of proceeds of the initial offering of Interests;

(n) do any act in contravention of this Agreement or which would make it impossible to carry on the business of the Fund;

(o) confess a judgment against the Fund in connection with any threatened or pending legal action;

(p) assign the rights of the Fund in specific Fund property for other than a Fund purpose;

(q) admit a person as a General Partner except with the consent of the Limited Partners or as otherwise provided for in this Agreement;

(r) intentionally perform any act (other than an act required by this Agreement) which would, at the time such act occurred, subject any Limited Partner to liability as a general partner in any jurisdiction;

(s) reinvest any Cash Available for Distribution or Sale or Refinancing Proceeds in real properties, except that Sale or Refinancing Proceeds may be reinvested, provided, that (i) the aggregate amount reinvested does not exceed 25% of the Gross Proceeds of the offering of Interests and (ii) cash proceeds from any Sale or Refinancing which occurs during the three-year period after the termination of the initial public offering of Interests may be reinvested in properties after sufficient amounts of such Sale or Refinancing Proceeds have been distributed to Taxable Investors to enable a Taxable Investor (assuming Taxable Investors are taxable at an overall 38% marginal rate) to pay the federal and state income tax created by such Sale or Refinancing;

(t) cause the Fund to pay any insurance brokerage fee to the General Partner or write any insurance policy covering the General Partner or any of the Fund properties, except that an Affiliate of the General Partner may provide insurance brokerage services to the Fund properties, except that an Affiliate of the General Partner may provide insurance brokerage services to the Fund if such Affiliate is independently engaged in the business of providing such services to other than Affiliates of the General Partner and at least 75% of such affiliate's insurance brokerage service gross revenues is derived from other than such Affiliates and provided that such Affiliate shall not be entitled to receive brokerage commissions in excess of the lowest quote obtained from two unaffiliated insurance agencies and the insurance coverage and terms are likewise comparable;

(u) employ, or permit to employ, the funds or assets of the Fund in any manner except for the benefit of the Fund;

(v) subject to any further restrictions on borrowings contained in this Agreement, incur any nonrecourse indebtedness wherein the lender will have or acquire, at any time as a result of making the loan, any direct or indirect interest in the profits, capital or property of the Fund other than as a secured creditor;

(w) subject to any further restrictions on borrowings contained in this Agreement, cause the Fund to incur aggregate borrowings in excess of 50% of the aggregate Purchase Price as to all Fund Properties;

(x) subject to any further restrictions on borrowings contained in this Agreement, and unless prior approval of the Department of Corporations of the State of California is obtained, cause the Fund to incur borrowings which, with level payments, would amortize such financing over a period in excess of 30 years. All such financing, including all-inclusive and wrap-around loans and interest-only loans, shall provide that no balloon payments may become due sooner than the earlier of: (a) ten years from the date the Fund acquires the property, or (b) two years beyond the anticipated holding period of the property, provided in such case that a balloon payment shall not become due sooner than seven years from the date the Fund acquires the property. The foregoing restrictions set forth in this paragraph (x) shall not apply to borrowings representing, in the aggregate, 25% or less of the total Purchase Price of the properties acquired;

(y) except as provided in Article 11.5 redeem or repurchase Interests on behalf of the Fund;

(z) commingle the funds of the Fund with those of any other person or entity except that such funds may be temporarily retained by property managers and except that funds of the Fund and funds of other partnerships sponsored by the General Partner or its Affiliates may be held in an account or accounts established and maintained for the purpose of making computerized disbursements and/or short-term investments; provided, however, that such funds are protected from claims of such other partnerships and/or their creditors;

(aa) except as permitted by Article VII and Sections 6.3(h), (n), (o) and (r) and 6.4(g), (h), (t) and (z), cause the Fund to enter into any transaction with any other partnership in which the General Partner or any Affiliate thereof has an interest, including, but not limited to, any transaction involving the sale, lease or purchase of any property to or from the Fund, the rendering of services to or from the fund, or the lending of any money or other property to or from the Fund;

(bb) directly or indirectly pay or award any finder's fee, commission or other compensation to any person engaged by a potential investor for investment advice as an inducement to such advisor to advise the purchaser regarding the purchase of Interests;

(cc) operate the Fund in such a manner as to have the Fund classified as an "investment company" for purposes of the Investment Company Act of 1940;

(dd) invest any of the Gross Proceeds in junior mortgages, junior deeds of trust or other similar obligations, except for junior mortgages or deeds of trust which are received by the Fund in connection with the Sale of a property;

(ee) cause the Fund to invest in (i) real estate contracts of sale (otherwise known as land sale contracts) unless such contracts of sale are in recordable form and are appropriately recorded in the chain of title, or (ii) invest in vacant land (unless incidental to the acquisition of a real estate investment);

(ff) cause the Fund to enter into any contract to construct major improvements to Fund property without one or more of the following: (a) retention of a reasonable portion of amounts payable to the general contractor as a potential offset in the event the general contractor does not perform in accordance with its construction contract; (b) such contract being guaranteed by a personal guarantee, accompanied by financial statements showing a substantial net worth provided by an individual associated with the person entering into the construction contract; (c) the general contractor guaranteeing performance at a fixed specified price, accompanied by financial statements of such general contractor which demonstrate the ability of the general contractor to perform under its guarantee; or (d) such contract being guaranteed at a fixed specified price by an adequate completion bond or other satisfactory arrangement;

(gg) cause the Fund to lend money or other assets to the General Partner or its Affiliates;

(hh) except as specifically provided for in Sections 6.3(a), (b), (h), (o), (r) and (u) and Sections 6.4(h), (dd) and (ee), cause the Fund to invest in or underwrite the securities of other issuers for any purpose; or (ii) invest more than 10% of the Gross Proceeds in properties which are non-income producing. For purposes of this paragraph (ii), properties which are expected to produce income within a period of six months after the acquisition thereof by the Fund shall not be considered non-income producing.

6.5 *Fund Business, Fiduciary Duty and Outside Activities.*

(a) The General Partner shall devote such time to Fund business as it, in its sole discretion, shall deem to be necessary to manage and supervise Fund business and affairs in an efficient manner; but nothing in this Agreement shall preclude the employment, at the expense of the Fund, of any agent or third party to manage or provide other services in respect of Fund property subject to the approval of the General Partner.

(b) The General Partner shall have a fiduciary responsibility for the safekeeping and use of all funds and assets of the Fund, whether or not in its immediate possession or control, and shall not employ or permit another to employ such funds or assets in any manner except for the exclusive benefit of the Fund. In addition, the Fund shall not permit the Interestholders to contract away the fiduciary duty owed to the Interestholders by the General Partner under common law.

Explanation: [The general partner is free to engage in other activities and may establish additional limited partnerships and serve as the general partner of these additional partnerships. This may create conflicts. The general partner, however, does agree not to set up competing partnerships until the funds raised in this offering are fully invested.]

(c) The General Partner shall not be required to manage the Fund as its sole and exclusive function and it may have other business interests and may engage in other activities in addition to those relating to the Fund, including the rendering of advice or services of any kind to other investors and the making or management of other investments. Neither the Fund nor any Partner or Assignee shall have any right by virtue of this Agreement or the partnership relationship created hereby in or to such other ventures or activities or to the income or proceeds derived therefrom and the pursuit of such ventures, even if competitive with the business of the Fund, shall not be deemed wrongful or improper unless these activities are inconsistent with the fiduciary duty of the General Partner to the Fund.

(d) To the extent that future affiliated partnerships have the same investment objectives and policies as the Fund, the General Partner will attempt to cause such affiliated partnerships not to acquire properties until substantially all of the Fund's Net Proceeds have been invested or committed for investment in properties (i.e., the Fund does not have sufficient Net Proceeds remaining to make an additional acquisition), unless an investment cannot be made by the Fund due to its investment objectives and policies or, in the interest of diversification or because of the size of the investment, the General Partner determines that the Fund should not take title to the property or the General Partner elects to have the Fund and such an affiliated partnership enter into a joint venture pursuant to Section 6.4(h). In the event that the Fund has funds available (because of a failure to consummate a proposed acquisition or otherwise) and any other subsequently formed partnership managed by the General Partner and/or its affiliates with similar investment objectives and policies has funds available at the same time for investment in the same or similar properties, conflicts of interest may arise as to which of the partnerships should proceed to acquire the property or properties involved. In such situations, the General Partner and its Affiliates will review the investment portfolio of each such partnership and will make the decision as to which such partnership will acquire the property on the basis of such factors as cash requirements of each partnership, the effect of the acquisition on diversification of each such partnership's portfolio, the estimated income tax effects of the purchase on each such partnership, the amount of funds available and the length of time such funds have been available for investment. If funds are available to two or more partnerships to purchase a given property or properties and the other factors enumerated above have been evaluated and deemed equally applicable to each partnership, then the General Partner and its Affiliates will acquire such properties for the partnerships on a rotating basis, commencing with the entity which has had funds available for investment for the longest period of time and so report to the partnership(s) not selected. In addition, the Fund is permitted to form joint ventures with other affiliated entities in accordance with Section 6.4(h).

6.6 *No Personal Liability*. The General Partner shall have no personal liability for the repayment of the Capital Contributions of any Interestholder or the repayment to the Fund of any portion or all of any negative balance in any Limited Partner's or Assignee's Capital Account, but shall have the liabilities set forth in Section 13.3. Nothing in this Section 6.6 shall be deemed to be in derogation of any of the provisions of Article XV hereof.

6.7 *Notice of Limitation of Liability*. The General Partner shall at all times conduct its affairs and the affairs of the Fund in such a manner that neither the Fund nor any Partner nor any Affiliate of any partner has any personal liability under any mortgage on any Fund properties, unless, in the opinion of the General Partner, it would be in the best interest of the Interestholders for the General Partner to incur such liability. The General Partner shall use its best efforts, in the conduct of the Fund's business, to put all suppliers and other persons with whom the Fund does business on notice that the Limited Partners are not liable for Fund obligations and all agreements to which the Fund is a party shall include a statement to the effect that the Fund is a limited partnership organized under Delaware law; but the General Partner shall not be liable to the Interestholders for any failure to give such notice to such suppliers or other persons or to include such a statement. Nothing in this Section 6.7 shall be deemed to be in derogation of any of the provisions of Article XV hereof.

6.8 *Investment in Properties; Return of Net Proceeds*. The Fund shall commit to Investment in Properties a percentage of Gross Proceeds equal to at least 87.5% of the Gross Proceeds. For this purpose, Gross Proceeds shall be reduced by any return of Net Proceeds to Interestholders. If the total amount of Front-End Fees must be reduced in order to enable the Fund to commit this percentage of the Gross Proceeds to Investment in Properties as required hereby, the General Partner shall, and shall cause its Affiliates or other persons to, reimburse the Fund for the amount of Front-End Fees received by them as necessary to enable the Fund to meet this investment requirement. Any Net Proceeds which are not invested or committed to investment (as provided in the Registration Statement) in real property within 24 months from the effective date of the Registration Statement shall be distributed to the Limited Partners as a return of Capital Contributions without reduction for Acquisition Fees which would have been payable if such funds had been invested in real properties. Such Net Proceeds will be available for general use of the Fund during such 24-month period and may be expended, utilized or set aside in the manner disclosed in the Registration Statement.

Explanation: [The general partner here agrees to limit up-front fees to 12.5 percent of what investors put up. For example, the general partner commits itself to assure that if an investor puts up $10,000, $8,750 will actually go into real estate assets for the partnership. If investors' money is not used to acquire real estate within 24 months, investors are entitled to a return of their uncommitted investment.]

6.9 *Accounting Matters*. The General Partner shall make all decisions as to account-ing matters in accordance with the accounting methods adopted by the Fund in accord-ance with generally accepted accounting principles and procedures applied on a consistent basis. The General Partner may rely on the Fund's independent certified public accountants to determine whether such decisions are in accordance with generally accepted accounting principles.

6.10 *Other Matters Concerning the General Partner*.

• • •

6.11 *Net Worth*. The General Partner shall maintain at all times substantial assets, other than its interest in the Fund and other limited partnerships in which it serves as general partner, of not less than $2,000,000 and shall use its best efforts to maintain sufficient net worth to preserve the Fund's classification as a partnership for federal income tax purposes in the event of any change in the Code, the Regulations or exist-ing interpretations thereof. The provisions of this Section 6.11 are intended for the benefit of the Partners and the Fund and shall not confer any right or claim upon or otherwise insure to the benefit of any creditor or other third parties having dealings with the Fund or the General Partner.

Explanation: [This provision assures that the general partner has sufficient as-sets so that the corporate characteristic of limited liability is avoided.]

ARTICLE VII
COMPENSATION AND REIMBURSEMENT OF THE GENERAL PARTNER AND AFFILIATES

7.1 *Compensation of the General Partner and Its Affiliates; Limitations*.

(a) The General Partner and its Affiliates shall receive compensation only as specified by this Agreement or as described in the Registration Statement.

Explanation: [These provisions are important in assessing a limited partner-ship. See the discussion in Chapter 9. Note that the general partner receives fees or compensation at the inception of the in-vestments made by the partnership, additional fees for manag-ing the partnership itself, additional fees for managing the property acquired by the partnership, and possibly additional fees when partnership property is sold. This is in addition to its 1 percent share of income from operations and 20 percent share of gain from sales of partnership property. Such fees are in no way unusual in a limited partnership, but rather, are quite customary.]

(b) The aggregate amount of Acquisition Fees and Investigatory Fees paid to all persons shall not exceed 6% of the Gross Proceeds; provided, however, in no event will Front-End Fees exceed 12-1/2% of the Gross Proceeds. In some situations, the payment of Acquisition Fees may be deferred, in which case the General Partner or its Affiliates may receive interest from the seller on the deferred amount. The interest rate paid on any such deferred Acquisition Fee will not exceed two percentage points over the prime lending rate charged by Citibank, New York, N.Y. In the event any Sale or Refinancing Proceeds are reinvested pursuant to Section 6.4(s), Acquisition Fees may be paid to the General Partner or Affiliates by any party, including the Fund, in connection with such reinvestment, provided the sum of such fee and the Acquisition Fee received on the initial acquisition by the General Partner or its Affiliates does not exceed the amount of Acquisition fees which could have been paid in connection with the initial acquisition.

(c) Except as set forth in this Article VII, no other real estate commission, property purchase fee, finder's fee or other fee or compensation shall be paid or payable by the Fund to the General Partner or to any other person in connection with the acquisition of specific properties; provided, however, that in the event such fees and other compensation exceed the limitations in this Section 7.1, the General Partner may cause such acquisition fees or other fee to be paid to other persons, which payments shall be without cost to the Fund and shall be borne by the General Partner out of its own assets.

7.2 *Nonaccountable Expense Allowance and Reimbursements.* In connection with the organization of the Fund and the offering and sale of Interests, the General Partner shall be entitled to receive from the Fund (a) a Nonaccountable Expense Allowance (for due diligence and marketing expenses) equal to 2% of the Gross Proceeds, provided such expense allowance shall be paid by the fund only to the extent that such payment does not result in increasing Organization and Offering Expenses over 6% of the Gross Proceeds; and (b) a reimbursement for advances made to cover Organization and Offering Expenses (including the Nonaccountable Expense Allowance) up to 6% of the Gross Proceeds, provided that the General Partner shall pay any Organization and Offering Expenses in excess of 6% of the Gross Proceeds.

7.3 *Acquisition and Investigatory Fees, Acquisition Expenses and Operating Cash Expenses.* The General Partner and its Affiliates shall be entitled to payment of Acquisition Fees and Investigatory Fees not exceeding the limitations specified in Section 7.1(b) and to reimbursement of any Acquisition Expenses and Operating Cash Expenses incurred by such entities on behalf of the Fund.

7.4 *Partnership Management Fee.* As compensation for services rendered in managing the affairs of the Fund, the General Partner shall be entitled to receive a partnership management fee which shall be in an amount equal to an aggregate of 9% of Cash Flow from Operations. The partnership management fee shall be paid following the end of each calendar quarter, but its payment shall be subordinated to the extent that Interestholders do not receive current noncumulative distributions from Cash Available for Distribution with respect to such quarter at a rate of 7% per annum on Interestholders' Adjusted Capital Contributions. If all or a portion of the fee is not paid by reason of such subordination, such unpaid fee or portion thereof shall not accrue or be paid in future quarters.

7.5 *Property Management Fee.* As compensation for property management or leasing services performed by the General Partner or any of its Affiliates with respect to any of the Fund properties (it being understood and agreed that the General Partner and Affiliates are not required to provide such services...), the Fund shall pay the General Partner or any of its Affiliates a property management or leasing fee. Any property management or leasing fees paid by the Fund to the General Partner or to any of its Affiliates shall be competitive in price and terms with those of nonaffiliated persons rendering similar services in the geographical area where the property is located and which could reasonably be made available to the Fund. Included in any such property management fee shall be bookkeeping services and fees paid to nonrelated persons for property management services. In no event shall any leasing fee be paid to the General Partner or to any of its Affiliates for performing leasing services unless the services are necessary for the leasing of space in a property and would be required to be performed for the Fund by a nonaffiliated person but for their performance by the General Partner or an Affiliate. Property management fees paid to the General Partner or any of its Affiliates shall not exceed the lesser of the following: the fees which are competitive for similar services in the same geographical area or 6% of the property's gross revenues.

• • •

7.6 *Real Estate Sales Commissions.* The General Partner or an Affiliate thereof may receive commissions if it provides substantial services in connection with the sale of properties by the Fund, which commissions will not exceed the lesser of 50% of amounts customarily charged in arm's length transactions by others rendering similar services for comparable properties or 3% of the sales price, provided that all real estate brokerage commissions or similar fees paid to all persons involved in the sale of any Fund property shall not exceed the lesser of amounts customarily charged in arm's-length transactions by others rendering similar services for comparable properties or 6% of the sales price (including the purchase price and all other cash payments paid to the Fund) of such property. The above limitations on real estate commissions to be received by the General Partner and its Affiliates are imposed by regulations of various state securities commissions. To the extent permitted by future change in such regulations as well as in the Guidelines, policies or procedures of the North American Securities Administrators Association, the above limitations may be reduced or eliminated. The commissions payable to the General Partner or an Affiliate are subordinated to the prior receipt by Interestholders of their Capital Contributions plus any deficiency in their Preferred Return through the end of the immediately preceding calendar quarter. If and to the extent that the General Partner or an Affiliate does not receive its commission due to the foregoing limitations, such commissions shall not be paid until the Interestholders shall have received their Capital Contributions plus their Preferred Return through the date of payment.

7.7 *Other Services.* Except as set forth in Article VII, Sections 6.3(h) (o), (r) and 64(t) and elsewhere in this Agreement, no other services may be performed by the General Partner or its Affiliates for the Fund except in circumstances where such services are required and are not readily available from an unaffiliated source at a reasonable price.

• • •

7.8 *Interest Upon Removal as General Partner.* Should the General Partner be removed from the Fund pursuant to the provisions of Article XII, any portion of Acquisition Fees, Acquisition Expenses, Nonaccountable Expense Allowance, Operating Cash Expenses, partnership management fee, real estate sales commissions, any interest in distributions of Cash Available for Distribution or Sale or Refinancing Proceeds, or any other fees or other compensation and reimbursable expense payable to the General Partner or any Affiliate according to the provisions of Articles V, VI and VII which are then accrued and due, but not yet paid, shall be paid by the Fund to the General Partner or such Affiliate in cash within 30 days of the date of removal as stated in the written notice of removal, unless such amount is included in the purchase price of the General Partner's interest in the Fund as determined in Section 12.5 hereof.

7.9 *Reimbursable Expenses.* All Fund expenses shall be billed directly to and paid by the Fund to the extent practicable. The General Partner and its Affiliates may be reimbursed for the Fund expenses as provided in Sections 7.2 and 7.3 and for the actual cost to the General Partner or any of its Affiliates of the Fund's Operating Cash Expenses.

• • •

7.10 *Nonreimbursable Expenses.* In addition to the exclusions from reimbursement set forth in the definition of Operating Cash Expenses in Article II, the General Partner and its Affiliates shall not be reimbursed by the Fund for Organization and Offering Expenses in excess of 6% of Gross Proceeds, payment of any such excess to be the obligation of the General Partner, which hereby agrees to pay the same.

7.11 *Payment of Partnership Expenses.* Subject to Sections 7.9 and 7.10, the Fund shall pay all costs and expenses and reimburse the actual cost to the General Partner or any of its Affiliates of the Fund's Operating Cash Expenses.

• • •

ARTICLE VIII
RIGHTS AND OBLIGATIONS OF INTERESTHOLDERS

8.1 *Limitation of Liability.* Except as provided below, a Limited Partner, as such, shall not be personally liable for any of the debts or obligations of the Fund or any of the losses of the Fund beyond the amount of its (or its predecessor's) Capital Contributions and its (or its predecessor's) share of the assets and undistributed profits of the Fund. Each Limited Partner shall be liable for the amount of any portion of such Capital Contribution returned to it, and for wrongful distributions received by it, to the extent set forth in the Delaware Act, and for taxes which the Fund may be required by law to pay and collect from it, but shall not be obligated to make any contribution to the Fund beyond the amount of the Capital Contribution for the Interests acquired by it (or it predecessor). The liability of an Assignee shall be the same as that of a Limited Partner as provided in the immediately preceding sentence.

Explanation: [The foregoing obligates a limited partner to the full amount of his agreed-to initial investment. If any distributions are a return of capital, a limited partner can be required to pay back this amount to the partnership if needed to satisfy partnership obligations. In no event can a limited partner be held liable for any amount in excess of his agreed-to initial capital contribution.]

8.2 *Management of Business.* No Interestholder (other than a General Partner, an Affiliate thereof or their directors, officers, partners, employees or agents in their capacity as such) shall take part in the operation, management or control (within the meaning of the Delaware Act) of the Fund's business, transact any business in the Fund's name or have the power to sign documents for or otherwise bind the Fund. The transaction of any such business by a director, trustee, officer, partner, employee or agent of a General Partner or an Affiliate thereof in its capacity as such shall not affect, impair or eliminate the limitations on the liability of any Interestholder under this Agreement.

8.3 *Outside Activities.* An Interestholder shall be entitled to and may have business interests and engage in business activities in addition to those relating to the Fund, including business interests and activities in direct competition with the Fund. Neither the Fund, any of the other Partners or Assignees nor any other person shall have any rights by virtue of this Agreement in any business ventures of any Interestholder or any of its revenues, profits or losses derived therefrom.

8.4 *Return of Capital.* No Interestholder shall be entitled to the withdrawal or return of his Capital Contribution, except to the extent, if any, that distributions made pursuant to this Agreement or upon termination of the Fund may be considered as such by law and then only to the extent provided for in this Agreement. Except as otherwise provided in Article V, no Interestholder shall have priority over any other Interestholder either as to the return of Capital Contributions or as to profits, losses or distributions.

Explanation: [In this partnership, investors cannot demand a return of their capital contributions.]

8.5 *Voting Rights.* Limited Partners shall have the right, by Majority Vote, to vote only upon the following matters affecting the basic structure of the Fund:

Explanation: [This list contains those matters over which limited partners have some control. For the most part, limited partners have few rights and generally are entitled to vote only on fundamental changes in the limited partnership which can alter their investment in a substantial way.]

(a) removal of the General Partner, provided that the removal of the last remaining General Partner shall not become effective until the election of a successor General Partner;

(b) election of any General Partner, including a successor General Partner and continuation of the business of the Fund pursuant to Section 13.1(c), provided, however, that any General Partner may, without the consent of any other General Partner or the Limited Partners to the extent permitted by law, (i) substitute in its stead as General Partner any entity which has, by merger, consolidation or otherwise, acquired substantially all of its assets, stock or other evidence of equity interest and continued its business, or (ii) cause to be admitted to the Fund an additional General Partner or Partners if it deems such admission to be necessary or desirable in order to provide a General Partner with a net worth of at least $2,000,000;

(c) termination, dissolution and winding up of the Fund;

(d) amendment of this Agreement as provided in Article XIV, except those amendments which the General Partner is empowered to make without a Majority Vote;

(e) approval or disapproval of a proposal to sell all or Substantially All of the Assets of the Fund in a single sale, or in multiple sales in the same 12- month period, except (i) sales in the ordinary course of the Fund's business, (ii) the sale of the Fund's final property, (iii) sales of mortgage loans acquired in connection with the sales of the Fund's real properties, and (iv) sales in the liquidation and winding up of the business of the Fund upon its termination and dissolution in the ordinary course of its business;

(f) pledge or encumbrance of all or Substantially All of the Assets of the Fund at one time;

(g) assignment of the General Partner's interest in the Fund except in connection with any merger, consolidation or sale as provided in paragraph (b) above and Sections 11.4, 12.4 and 12.8;

(h) the extension of the term of the Fund;

(i) a material alteration of the nature of the business of the Fund as set forth in Article III or a material change in the three principal investment objectives of the Fund, as described in the prospectus contained in the Registration Statement;

(j) a material modification of any contract entered into pursuant to Section 7.7 which may be adverse to the Fund or the Interestholders; and

(k) a reconstitution of the Fund pursuant to Section 10.8.

Explanation: [The following provisions essentially spell out the procedure limited partners can follow in order to remove the general partner.]

8.6 *Meetings; Notices.* The General Partner may at any time call a meeting of the Limited Partners or for a vote, without a meeting, of the Limited Partners on matters upon which they are entitled to vote, and shall call for such meeting or vote following receipt of written request therefor by Limited Partners holding 10% or more of the Interests held by all Limited Partners as of the date of receipt of such written request ("notice date"). Within 10 days of such notice date, the General Partner shall notify all Limited Partners of record as of the notice date as to the time and place of the Fund meeting, if called, and the general nature of the business to be transacted thereat including a verbatim statement of the wording of any resolution proposed for adoption by the Limited Partners and of any proposed admedment to the Agreement, or if no such meeting has been called, of the matter or matters to be voted upon and the date upon which the votes will be counted. Any Fund meeting or the date upon which such votes, without a meeting, will be counted (regardless of whether the General Partner has called for such meeting at the request of Limited Partners or has initiated such event without such request) shall be no less than 15 nor more than 60 days following mailing of the notice thereof by the General Partner. All expenses of the voting and such notification shall be borne by the Fund. If a meeting is adjourned to another time or place, and if an announcement of the adjournment of time or place is made at the meeting, it shall not be necessary to give any notice of the adjourned meeting. The presence in person or by proxy of a majority in interest of the Limited Partners shall constitute a quorum at all meetings of the Limited Partners; provided, however, that if there be no such quorum, holders of a majority in interest of the Limited Partners present may adjourn the meeting from time to time without further notice, until a quorum shall have been obtained. No notice of the time, place or purpose of any meeting of Limited Partners need be given to (a) any Limited Partner who attends in person or is represented by proxy, except for a Limited Partner attending a meeting for the express purpose of objecting at the beginning of the meeting to the transaction of any business on the ground that the meeting is not lawfully called or convened, or (b) any Limited Partner entitled to such notice who, in writing, executed and filed with the records of the meeting, either before or after the time thereof, waives such notice.

8.7 *Voting Procedures.* A Limited Partner shall be entitled to cast one vote for each Interest that he owns: (a) at a meeting, in person, by written proxy or by a signed writing directing the manner in which he desires that his vote be cast, which writing must be received by the General Partner prior to such meeting, or (b) without a meeting, by a signed writing, directing the manner in which he desires that his vote be cast, which writing must be received by the General Partner prior to the date upon which the votes of Limited Partners of record on the notice date, whether at a meeting or otherwise, shall be counted. The General Partner shall not be entitled to vote unless and to the extent it owns Interests. The laws of the State of Delaware pertaining to the validity and use of corporate proxies shall govern the validity and use of proxies given by Limited Partners. At each meeting of Limited Partners, the General Partner shall appoint such officers and adopt such rules for the conduct of such meeting as the General Partner shall deem appropriate. In connection with each meeting or vote without a meeting of the Limited Partners, the Fund shall provide for proxies or written consents which specify a choice between approval and disapproval of each matter to be acted upon at the meeting or by vote without a meeting. For purposes of obtaining a written vote under this Agreement, the General Partner may require a written response within a specified time, but not less than 15 days nor more than 60 days following the mailing of notice thereof by the General Partner.

8.8 *Limitations.* No Interestholder shall have the right or power to: (a) bring an action for partition against the Fund; (b) cause the termination and dissolution of the Fund by court decree or otherwise, except as set forth in this Agreement or as provided by law; or (c) demand or receive property other than cash in return for his contribution. Other than upon the termination and dissolution of the Fund as provided by this Agreement, there has been no time agreed upon when the contribution of each Interestholder may be returned.

8.9 *Rights of Interestholders Relating to Fund Books and Records.*

(a) Each Interestholder shall have the right for a proper purpose reasonably related to such Interestholder's interest as a holder of Interests in the Fund, within a reasonable period of time and with notice and at such Interestholder's own expense (except as otherwise provided below):

(i) to obtain true and full information regarding the status of the business and financial condition of the Fund;

(ii) promptly after becoming available, to obtain a copy of the Fund's federal, state and local income tax returns for each year;

(iii) to have furnished to him, upon notification to the General Partner, a current list of the name and last known mailing address of each Partner and Assignee;

(iv) at the Fund's expense, to have furnished to him, upon notification to the General Partner, a copy of this Agreement and the Certificate of Limited Partnership and all amendments thereto;

(v) copies of any executed powers of attorney pursuant to which this Agreement, the Certificate of Limited Partnership and all amendments thereto have been executed; and

(vi) to inspect and copy any of the Fund's books and records and obtain such other information regarding the affairs of the Fund as is just and reasonable.

(b) Notwithstanding the other provisions hereof, the General Partner may keep confidential from the Interestholders for such period of time as the General Partner deems reasonable, any information which the General Partner reasonably believes to be in the nature of trade secrets or other information which the Fund is required by law to keep confidential, or, except to the extent information is sought solely for a proper purpose reasonably related to an Interestholder's interest as a holder of Interests in the Fund and not for the prupose of commercial use or other competitive reasons, other information the disclosure of which the General Partner in good faith believes is not in the best interests of the Fund or in good faith believes could damage the Fund or its business or which the Fund is required by agreements with third parties to keep confidential.

ARTICLE IX
BOOKS OF ACCOUNT, RECORDS AND REPORTS

9.1 *Books and Records*. Proper and complete records and books of account shall be kept by the General Partner.

• • •

9.2 *Valuation of Interests*. The General Partner shall, within 90 days following the close of the last quarter of each fiscal year, send to each person who was an Interestholder at any time during the fiscal year then ended an evaluation of its interest in the Fund.

• • •

9.3 *Quarterly Reports*. Within 60 days after the end of the first three quarters of each fiscal year, the General Partner shall send to each person who was an Interestholder at any time during the quarter then ended the following (none of which need be audited): (i) a balance sheet, (ii) a profit and loss statement, (iii) a statement of changes in financial position, (iv) other pertinent information regarding the Fund and its activities during the quarter covered by the report.

9.4 *Tax Information*. Within 75 days after the end of each calendar year, the General Partner shall send to each person who was an Interestholder at any time during the fiscal year then ended such tax information as shall be necessary for the preparation by such holder of his federal income tax return, and state income and other tax returns with regard to jurisdictions in which the Fund is formed or qualified.

9.5 *Annual Reports.* Within 120 days after the end of each fiscal year, the General Partner shall send to each person who was an Interestholder at any time during the fiscal year then ended (i) a balance sheet as of the end of such fiscal year and statements of income, partners' equity and changes in financial position for such fiscal year, all of which shall be prepared in accordance with generally accepted accounting principles and accompanied by an independent accountant's report, (ii) a report containing a breakdown of the costs reimbursed to the General Partner and its Affiliates and summarizing the fees and other remuneration paid by the Fund for such fiscal year to the General Partner or any Affiliate thereof, (iii) a report of the activities of the Fund during such fiscal year, and (iv) a statement (which need not be audited) showing the Cash Available for Distribution and Sale or Refinancing Proceeds distributed to Interestholders in respect of such year.

9.6 *Special Reports.* The General Partner shall have prepared, at fund expense, as of the end of each quarter following the termination of the offering in which the Fund contracts to acquire properties, a special report which shall provide the information contained in all Form 8-K filings with the Securities and Exchange Commission relating to such contracts.

• • •

9.7 *Reduction of Reporting Requirements.* In the event that the Securities and Exchange Commission or the North American Securities Administrators Association promulgates rules which allow a reduction in the Fund's reporting requirements, the Fund may cease preparing and filing certain of the aforementioned reports if the General Partner determines such action to be in the best interests of the Fund.

• • •

9.9 *Filing Reports with Governmental Entities.* The General Partner, at Fund expense, shall have authority to cause to be prepared and filed, with appropriate federal and state regulatory and administrative bodies, all reports required to be filed with such entities under the current applicable laws, rules and regulations. Such reports shall be prepared on the accounting or reporting basis required by such regulatory bodies.

ARTICLE X
TAX MATTERS

10.1 *Preparation of Tax Returns.* The General Partner shall arrange for the preparation and timely filing of all returns of Fund income, gains, deductions, losses and other items necessary for federal and state income tax purposes. The classification, realization and recognition of income, gain, losses and deductions and other iterms initially shall be on the accrual method of accounting for federal income tax purposes. The taxable year of the Fund shall be the calendar year, unless the General Partner shall determine otherwise in its sole discretion.

10.2 *Tax Elections*. Except as otherwise provided herein, the General Partner shall, in its sole discretion, determine whether to make any available election pursuant to the Code. The General Partner shall have the right to seek to revoke any such election upon the General Partner's determination that such revocation is in the best interests of the Interestholders.

10.3 *Tax Matters Partners*. Subject to the provisions hereof, the General Partner is designated the Tax Matters Partner.

• • •

Explanation: [The Tax Matters Partner represents the partnership in its dealings with the Internal Revenue Service. The Internal Revenue Code requires most partnerships to designate a Tax Matters Partner.]

• • •

10.4 *Organizational Expenses and Pre-Opening Costs*. The Fund shall elect to deduct expenses incurred in organizing the Fund ratably over a 60-month period as provided in Section 709 of the Code. The fund shall elect to amortize expenses that are pre-opening costs over a 60-month period as provided in Section 195 of the Code.

10.5 *Taxation as a Partnership*.

• • •

ARTICLE XI
ASSIGNMENT OF INTERESTS BY AND SUBSTITUTION OF LIMITED PARTNERS; OPTIONAL REPURCHASE OF INTERESTS

11.1 *Assignment*. An Interestholder may transfer and assign all or any portion of his Interests, as the case may be, after the Termination Date (but only in whole Interests) in the following manner and subject to the following conditions:

Explanation: [The following provisions are intended to allow limited partners to sell or assign their interests, but only to a limited extent. The general partner reserves the right to refuse to recognize transfers that would make the partnership a "publicly traded partnership" under the tax law or otherwise affect the classification of the limited partnership as a partnership.]

(i) An instrument of assignment executed by both the assignor and the assignee of the Interests satisfactory in form to the General Partner shall be delivered to the General Partner along with a transfer fee which is sufficient to cover all actual, necessary and reasonable expenses not to exceed $150 per transaction in connection with the assignment or transfer of Interests (the $150 limitation may be increased by the General Partner to such amount as it deems necessary by giving notice of such increase to the Interestholders in an annual or quarterly report made pursuant to Article IX of the Agreement).

(ii) Each assignment shall be effective as of the last day of the quarter during which the General Partner actually receives the instrument of assignment.

• • •

(iii) The effectiveness of any assignment may be deferred if the General Partner determines that the deferral is necessary or appropriate for federal income tax purposes.

(iv) The General Partner may refuse to recognize the effectiveness of a transfer or assignment in a secondary market (or the substantial equivalent thereof) if the General Partner determines that recognition of the effectiveness of such transfer or assignment might cause the Fund to be treated as "publicly traded" for purposes of Sections 469, 512 and 7704 of the Code.

(v) No assignment shall be effective if such assignment would, in the opinion of the General Partner supported by an opinion of counsel, result in the termination of the Fund for pusposes of the then applicable provisions of the Code.

(vi) No assignment shall be effective if the assignment would, to the knowledge of the General Partner, violate the provisions of any applicable state securities law.

(vii) No assignment to a minor or incompetent shall be effective in any respect.

Any such assignment shall confer upon the assignee the right to become a substituted Limited Partner subject to the written consent of the General Partner, which consent may be granted or denied in the sole and absolute discretion of the General Partner. This right is provided to the General Partner for the purpose of maintaining the tax status of the Fund and to insure compliance with applicable law. Prior to the giving of such consent by the General Partner, such substitution shall not be effective. The written consent or a notice of denial of consent shall be given to the assignee within thirty days following the effectiveness of the assignment.

11.2 *Filings.* The General Partner shall execute, file and record with the appropriate governmental agencies such documents (including amendments to this Agreement) as are required to reflect such substitution.

• • •

11.3 *Effect of Assignment and Substitution.* An Assignee shall be entitled to receive allocations of net income, net loss and distributions from the Fund attributable to such Interests from and after the effective date of the assignment of such Interests.

• • •

Any assignee and any person admitted to the Fund as a substituted Limited Partner pursuant to this Article XI shall be subject to and bound by all the provisions of this Agreement as if originally a party to this Agreement.

11.4 *Assignment by the General Partner.* The General Partner shall have the right to sell, assign and transfer a portion of its interest in income, gains, losses, deductions, credits and distributions of the Fund to a partnership for the benefit of certain employees of the General Partner and its Affiliates.

• • •

Notwithstanding the foregoing, no assignment under this Section 11.4 shall constitute a transfer of the General Partner's Partnership Interest as a General Partner, and the General Partner shall continue as a General Partner hereunder.

11.5 *Optional Repurchase of Interests.* The General Partner, in its sole discretion, may repurchase Interests from existing Interestholders from amounts it may set aside for such purpose, provided that no such repurchase may be made if as a result thereof such Interestholder would continue to be an Interestholder and would hold less than 10 Interests and provided further that in no event will the Interestholder be permitted to have its Interests repurchased prior to January 1, 1990, upon the terms and conditions hereinafter set forth provided further that no such repurchase shall be made except in case of death, divorce, disability, insolvency or other similar circumstance where the General Partner determines, at its sole discretion, that liquidity is necessary, unless the General Partner has received an opinion of counsel to the effect that the repurchase of Interests pursuant to the Section will not cause the Fund to be treated as "publicly traded" for purposes of Sections 469, 512 and 7704 of the Code.

Explanation: [The general partner may repurchase partnership interests from investors in the limited circumstances described. The detailed procedure involved in requesting repurchase and making repurchases has been omitted.]

• • •

ARTICLE XII
WITHDRAWAL AND REMOVAL OF THE GENERAL PARTNER;
TRANSFER OF INTEREST

12.1 *No Voluntary Dissolution or Withdrawal.* Except as provided in Section 12.6, until the dissolution of the Fund, the General Partner shall not take any voluntary step to dissolve itself or to withdraw from the Fund.

12.2 *Removal.* The General Partner may be removed from the Fund upon a Majority Vote pursuant to the provisions of Section 8.5(a). The removal of a General Partner shall in no way impair any rights of such General Partner pending the effective date of such removal and the election of its replacement.

12.3 *Notice.* Written notice of a removal of the General Partner shall be served upon the General Partner either by certified or by registered mail, return receipt requested, or by personal service. Such notice shall set forth the date upon which the removal is to become effective.

12.4 *Sale of Interest.* Upon the removal, Bankruptcy, dissolution or other cessation to exist of the General Partner and the continuation of the business of the Fund, the interest of the General Partner in the items of income and loss and distributions of the Fund shall be purchased by the Fund for a purchase price determined according to the provisions of Section 12.5.

12.5 *Purchase Price.* Upon the occurrence of an event as set forth in Section 12.4, the General Partner shall receive from the Fund the fair market value of its interest in the Fund.

• • •

12.6 *Transfers.* The General Partner's interest in the Fund shall not be transferred, except in connection with any merger, consolidation, assignment or sale as provided in Sections 8.5(b), 11.4, 12.4 or 12.8, without a Majority Vote. Any entity to which the entire interest of the General Partner in the Fund is transferred in compliance with Section 8.5(b), Section 12.8 and this Section 12.6 shall be substituted by the General Partner by the filing of appropriate amendments to the Agreement and the Certificate of Limited Partnership of the Fund, as theretofore amended, in its stead as a General Partner of the Fund.

12.7 *Report after Removal.* Within 90 days after the Limited Partners have voted to remove a General Partner, the successor General Partner, if any, shall prepare, at Fund expense, a financial statement (balance sheet, statement of income or loss, partners' equity and changes in financial positions) prepared in accordance with generally accepted accounting principles and accompanied by a report thereon containing an opinion of an independent certified public accounting firm of recognized standing and shall cause such statement to be mailed to Interestholders as soon as possible after receipt thereof.

12.8 *No Limitation on Merger.* Nothing in this Agreement shall be deemed to prevent the assignment by the General Partner of its economic interest in the Fund or the merger or reorganization of the General Partner into or with any other corporation, or the transfer of all the capital stock of the General Partner and the assumption of the rights and duties of the General partner by, in the case of a merger, reorganization or consolidation, the surviving corporation by operation of law. Each Limited Partner and Assignee hereby consents to any such assignment or transfer by the General Partner.

ARTICLE XIII
DISSOLUTION AND LIQUIDATION

13.1 *Dissolution.* The Fund shall not be dissolved by the admission of substituted or additional Limited Partners or by the admission of substituted or additional General Partners in accordance with the terms of this Agreement. Upon the removal, withdrawal or resignation of any General Partner, any remaining General Partner and any substituted General Partner may continue the business of the fund without dissolution. The Fund shall dissolve, and its affairs shall be wound up, upon:

(a) the expiration of its term as provided in Section 1.5;

(b) a Majority Vote of the Limited Partners to dissolve the Fund as provided in Section 8.5(c);

(c) the withdrawal, removal, Bankruptcy, dissolution or other cessation to exist as a legal entity of the General Partner, unless (i) the remaining General Partners, if any, within 90 days of the date of such event, elect to continue the business of the Fund, or (ii) if there are no remaining General Partners, within 90 days of the date of such event, the Limited Partners by Majority Vote, if permitted by applicable law, elect a successor General Partner effective as of the date of such event and elect to continue the business of the Fund, in a reconstituted form if necessary. Any reconstitution of the Fund shall be in accordance with Section 13.2 below. Expenses incurred in such reconstitution, or the attempted reconstitution, of the Fund shall be deemed expenses of the Fund;

(d) the disposition of all interests in real property and other assets of the Fund and the receipt of the final payment of the sales price of all such real property and assets; or

(e) the election by the General Partner to terminate the Fund, without the consent of any Interestholder, in the event that either (a) the Fund's assets constitute "plan assets," as such term is defined for purposes of ERISA, or (b) any material transaction contemplated by this Agreement constitutes a "prohibited transaction" under ERISA and no exemption for such transaction is obtainable from the United States Department of Labor or the General Partner determines not to seek such an exemption;

(f) the happening of an event which makes it unlawful for the Fund to continue its business.

Glossary

Accounting Return: The total profit from an investment divided by the cost of the investment, with the result divided by the number of years of investment.

Accredited Investor: An investor who meets standards imposed by the SEC and therefore does not need the full protection of the federal securities laws.

Accrued-Interest Mortgage: Similar to zero-coupon debt. When accrued-interest financing is used, the borrower agrees to a higher overall rate of interest, but is obligated to actually pay some lower amount for an initial period with the rest of the interest compounding until maturity.

Agreement of Limited Partnership: The legal contract between the members of the partnership. Controls the relationships among the limited and general partners within the partnership and spells out what the general partners are agreeing to do on behalf of the limited partners. It is the document that stipulates the rights and obligations of the general and limited partners with respect to each other.

Appreciation: The actual rise in the value of an investment because values increase over time, because of growth, or because of the actual activity of managing or operating the investment, such as the discovery of oil in an oil and gas limited partnership.

At-Risk Rule: A tax rule that limits deductions from an activity to income from the activity, plus deductions in excess of income to the extent the investor has invested money or is personally liable for borrowed amounts.

Blind Pool: An offering that does not specify the specific properties to be acquired at the time funds are raised from investors.

Blue-Sky Laws: State securities laws are often referred to as "Blue-Sky" laws, because of the penchant of some unscrupulous promoters before the days of securities regulation for selling unsuspecting investors pieces of the great blue sky above, and very little of substance.

Capital Account: A partner's capital account measures the partner's adjusted investment in the partnership, that is, what that partner would receive at any given moment if the partnership were liquidated.

Cash Flow: The actual after-tax cash distributed to or realized by a limited partner while he holds his interest and upon the liquidation of the partner's interest in the partnership.

Certificate of Limited Partnership: Document filed with state authorities to acquire the status of a limited partnership. Filing this certificate is closely akin to the filing of articles of incorporation by a corporation and its primary purpose is to protect potential creditors of the partnership by informing them of the business and financial status of the partnership organization.

General Partnership: A partnership in which all the partners share equally in the right to conduct the business of the partnership and in which all partners are also jointly and severally liable to third parties for the obligations of the partnership and the acts of agents and employees of the partnership.

Guaranteed Payment: Limited partners, or a class of limited partners, may be guaranteed a minimum return based on the amount of their initial capital contributions regardless of the income of the partnership. These guaranteed payments which are made without regard to partnership income are ordinary income to the recipient partners; in effect, guaranteed payments for the use of partners' capital are in the nature of interest and are treated as such for tax purposes.

Internal Rate of Return (IRR): The discount rate that, when applied to an investment, results in the sum of the present values (PV) of the costs and the benefits of the investment equaling zero.

Intrastate Offering: An offering of securities entirely within a single state when the issuer, the business, and all purchasers are within the state and which is exempt from SEC registration.

Investment Advisor: Any person who, for compensation, engages in the business of advising others, either directly or through publications or writings, as to the value of securities or as to the advisability of investing in, purchasing, or selling securities, or who, for compensation and as part of a regular business, issues or promulgates analyses or reports concerning securities.

Investment Advisors Act: This act requires anyone who comes within the definition of an "investment advisor" to register with the SEC.

Investment Contract: A security that has the following characteristics: an investment in a common enterprise by investors seeking to profit through the skill and efforts of others.

Kiddie Tax: The tax imposed on the unearned income of children under the age of 14 at their parents' marginal tax rate.

Leverage: The use of debt or borrowed funds to obtain an economic or financial advantage.

Limited Partnership: A partnership in which one or more partners have their liability limited in much the same fashion as shareholders in a corporation have their liability limited. In a limited partnership, there must be at least one general partner. The general partner or partners manage the business and are personally liable for the obligations of the partnership. The limited partners in a limited partnership are exempt from partnership liability for the debts, obligations, and losses of the partnership as long as they do not participate in the management of the partnership.

Limited Partnership Agreement: See "Agreement of Limited Partnership."

Master Limited Partnership (MLP): A limited partnership in which interests are publicly traded through listings on a stock exchange or in the over-the-counter market.

National Association of Securities Dealers (NASD): A self-regulatory body of securities brokers and dealers engaged in the over-the-counter securities market. The goal of the NASD is to promote fair practice by its members within the securities industry.

Net Present Value: The sum of all costs and benefits converted to their present value (PV) at some assumed interest rate.

No-Load Limited Partnerships: Public partnership programs that are offered to the general public directly by the general partner or sponsor of the program, usually through direct mail.

Non-recourse Financing: Loans for which the borrower has no personal liability. The lender must look only to property financed by the loans for security.

Organization and Syndication Costs: The costs of organizing and syndicating a limited partnership are not immediately deductible in computing the taxable income of the partnership. The actual costs of organizing a limited partnership must be charged to a capital account and then deducted over a period of at least 60 months. The costs of syndicating a limited partnership, generally all the expenses involved in selling partnership interests to investors, are not deductible at all.

Partnership: An association of two or more persons for the purpose of carrying on a business for profit as co-owners.

Passive Loss Rule: A tax rule that essentially provides that losses from "passive activities" can be used only to offset income from passive activities and tax credits generated by passive activities can be used only to offset tax liability attributable to passive activities.

Payback Period: The time required for the after-tax income from the investment to equal the after-tax cost of the investment.

Phantom Income: Taxable income in excess of cash distributions or cash flow from an investment.

Private Offering: A private offering or "private placement" under Reguation D is an offering of securities to not more than 35 individuals who are not "accredited investors."

Profit and Loss Sharing Ratio: The share of each partner in the profits or losses of the partnership as set forth in the partnership agreement.

Prospectus: Any written or broadcast material that offers a security for sale to the public. It is the term applied to the sales documents for a security that is registered with the SEC under the Securities Act of 1933.

Public Limited Partnership: A limited partnership that is registered with the SEC and which has units that are offered for sale to the public.

Publicly Traded Partnership: A partnership in which the interests are traded on an established securities market, or readily tradable on a secondary market or the substantial equivalent of a secondary market.

Racketeer Influenced and Corrupt Organizations Act (RICO): A statute which was enacted by Congress as a weapon against organized crime and which, in addition to various criminal sanctions, authorizes private lawsuites by aggrieved individuals to recover treble damages plus costs and attorney's fees

Index